COMPASSION

THE GREAT HEALER'S ART

COMPASSION

THE GREAT HEALER'S ART

ULISSES SOARES

DESERET BOOK

© 2023 Ulisses Soares

All rights reserved. No part of this book may be reproduced in any form or by any means without permission in writing from the publisher, Deseret Book Company, at permissions@deseretbook.com. This work is not an official publication of The Church of Jesus Christ of Latter-day Saints. The views expressed herein are the responsibility of the author and do not necessarily represent the position of the Church or of Deseret Book Company.

DESERET BOOK is a registered trademark of Deseret Book Company.

Visit us at deseretbook.com

Library of Congress Cataloging-in-Publication Data
(CIP data on file)
ISBN 978-1-63993-137-8

Printed in the United States of America
Publishers Printing, Salt Lake City, UT

10 9 8 7 6 5 4 3 2 1

CONTENTS

Introduction 1

1. The Savior's Abiding Compassion 5
2. Joy and Peace in Him 17
3. Being Meek and Lowly of Heart 33
4. Ministering to All 43
5. Loving Those Who Are Different from Us 61
6. Always Remember Him 73
7. Learning and Teaching the Gospel 87
8. Scriptures and Prophets: Testaments of Christ's Love . . . 97
9. The Gift of Repentance 121
10. Taking Up Our Cross and Following Him 135
11. Paths for Happiness 147

    Conclusion 161

    Acknowledgments 164

    Notes 167

    Image Credits 170

INTRODUCTION

In the classic movie *Amazing Grace*, William Wilberforce is a British politician, philanthropist, and leader of the movement to abolish the slave trade and reform the education system. In one memorable scene, his friend asked him, "You don't believe you and I could change things?" Then William Wilberforce wisely answered, "I would change myself first."

Like that friend, we are sometimes full of the desire to do something good, and we can easily recognize the need for change in the world around us. And sometimes we have a perspective more like that of Wilberforce. He also had righteous goals and ambitions, but he wanted first to align his desires with the Lord's—to change himself first before he worked to enact change around him. William Wilberforce had a heart full of compassion and lived his life trying to give freedom to his friends, his brothers and sisters in Christ.

Compassion is an attribute of our Savior, Jesus Christ, and is a gift of the Spirit. It has its roots in the second great commandment: "Thou shalt love thy neighbour as thyself" (Matthew 22:39). It merges with other Christlike attributes such as long-suffering, mildness, meekness, goodness, and especially the Golden Rule taught by the Savior in the Sermon on the Mount—"Therefore all things whatsoever ye would that [men and women] should do to you, do ye even so to them" (Matthew 7:12).

In His mercy and love, the Lord, who gives liberally, invites us to seek earnestly the best gifts in all holiness of heart, walking uprightly before Him, doing all things with prayer and thanksgiving. The Lord said: "Seek ye earnestly the best gifts, always remembering for what they are given; for verily I say unto you, they are given for the benefit of those who love me and keep all my commandments" (Doctrine and Covenants 46:8–9). We receive the best gifts when we selflessly use them to serve our Heavenly Father's children. What a blessing it is to be the Lord's hands in serving our brothers and sisters.

I invite you to join with me in examining compassion as a gift of the Spirit that can be acquired by all who seek to be like Christ. In this book, we will explore Christ's perfect example of compassion in ways that are applicable to us, personally. We will also consider how we can daily emulate Christ's compassion as we love and serve one another as the Savior did. There are countless ways in which He shows love, and just as many ways that we can demonstrate our compassion for others and our gratitude for Him. Our Savior's life was full of examples that teach us how to show compassion for those who are in need.

When Jesus appeared to His people in the Americas, as recorded in 3 Nephi 17:7, He addressed the people and made the following invitation: "Have ye any that are sick among you? Bring them hither. Have ye any that are lame, or blind, or halt, or maimed, or leprous, or that are withered, or that are deaf, or that are afflicted in any manner? Bring them hither and I will heal them, for I have compassion upon you; my bowels are filled with mercy."

This beautiful, healing invitation is extended even today. We each have the opportunity to come unto the Savior and receive the divine compassion that is so needed in our world. As we partake of the compassionate gifts the Savior has offered us—including guidance and direction for this life, a way to return to Him in the next life, scriptures, the invitation to repent, commandments to follow Him, and so many more—we are better able to share His compassion with those around us. When we practice compassion for our fellow man, we practice the Great Healer's art, helping to seal up wounds and divisions that might otherwise fester and injure. Like William Wilberforce, we can learn to align our own hearts to the Savior's so that we are ready to act as His hands on earth.

Chapter 1

THE SAVIOR'S ABIDING COMPASSION

The Gospel of Luke relates that a certain woman, considered a sinner, entered the home of Simon, a Pharisee, while Jesus was there. In humble contrition, the woman approached Jesus, washed His feet with her tears, wiped them with her hair, and then kissed them and anointed them with a special ointment (see Luke 7:36–39). The proud host, who considered himself morally superior to the woman, thought to himself with reproach and arrogance, "This man, if he were a prophet, would have known who and what manner of woman this is that toucheth him: for she is a sinner" (Luke 7:39).

The Pharisee's holier-than-thou attitude led him to judge unjustly both Jesus and the woman. But in His omniscience, the Savior knew Simon's mind and, in great wisdom, challenged Simon's condescending attitude and admonished him for his lack of courtesy in receiving a special guest like the Savior into his home. In fact, Jesus's direct rebuke of the Pharisee served as a witness that Jesus was indeed a prophet and that this woman, with a humble and contrite heart, was repentant and forgiven for her sins (see Luke 7:40–50).

Like many other events during Jesus's earthly ministry, this account demonstrates once more that the Savior acted compassionately toward all who would come unto Him—without distinction—especially toward those who most needed His help. The contrition and reverent love shown to Jesus by the woman were evidence of her sincere repentance and desire to receive a remission of her sins. However, Simon's hardened heart prevented him from showing empathy for that repentant soul, and he even treated the Savior of the world with indifference and contempt. His attitude revealed that his way of life was nothing more than a strict and hollow observance of rules—outward manifestations of his convictions through self-aggrandizement and false holiness.

The compassionate and personalized ministering of Jesus in this account demonstrates a perfect model of how we should interact with our neighbor. The scriptures have countless examples of how the Savior, moved by His deep and abiding compassion, interacted with people of His day and helped those who were suffering and those who had "fainted, and were scattered abroad, as sheep having no shepherd" (Matthew 9:36). He extended His merciful hand to those who needed relief from their burdens, both physically and spiritually.

The compassionate attitude of Jesus is rooted in charity, namely, in His pure and perfect love, which is foundational to His atoning sacrifice. Compassion is a fundamental characteristic of those who strive for sanctification, and this divine quality intertwines with other Christlike traits such as mourning with those who mourn and having empathy, mercy, and kindness. The expression of compassion for others is, in fact, an essential aspect of the gospel of Jesus Christ and a marked evidence of our spiritual and emotional closeness to the Savior. Furthermore, it shows the level of influence we allow Him to have on our way of life and demonstrates the magnitude of our spirits.

It is meaningful to observe that Jesus's compassionate acts were not occasional or mandated manifestations based on a list of tasks to be completed but everyday expressions of the reality of His pure love for God and His children and His abiding desire to help them.

Jesus was able to identify people's needs even at a distance. Thus, it is not surprising, for example, that immediately after healing a certain centurion's servant, Jesus traveled from Capernaum to the city called Nain (see Luke 7:1–10). It was there that Jesus performed one of the most tender miracles of His earthly ministry when He commanded a dead young man, the only son of a widowed mother, to rise and live. Jesus sensed not only the intense suffering of that poor mother but also the difficult circumstances of her life, and He was moved by genuine compassion for her (see Luke 7:11–15).

Just like the sinful woman and the widow of Nain, many people within our circle of influence are seeking comfort, acknowledgment, inclusion, and any help that we can offer them. We all can be instruments in the Lord's hands and act compassionately toward those in need, just as Jesus did.

I know a little girl who was born with very serious cleft lips and a cleft palate. She had to have the first of a series of many surgeries on the second day of her life. Moved by a genuine compassion for those who experience this same challenge, this girl and her parents seek to give support, understanding, and emotional assistance to others who face this difficult reality. They wrote to me once and shared: "Through our daughter's challenge, we had the opportunity to meet wonderful people who needed comfort, support, and encouragement. Some time ago, our daughter, who is eleven years old now, talked with the parents of a baby with the same challenge. During this conversation, our daughter momentarily took off the mask she was wearing due to the pandemic so the parents could see that there is hope, even though that baby still has a long way to go in the next few years to fix the problem. We feel very grateful for the opportunity to extend our empathy to those who suffer, as the Savior does for us. We feel we ease our pain every time we relieve someone else's pain."

As we intentionally strive to incorporate a compassionate attitude into our way of life, as exemplified by the Savior, we will become more sensitive to people's needs. With that increased sensitivity, feelings of genuine interest and love will permeate our every action. The Lord will recognize our efforts, and we will surely be blessed with opportunities to be instruments in His hands in softening hearts and in bringing relief to those whose "hands . . . hang down" (Doctrine and Covenants 81:5).

Jesus's admonition to Simon the Pharisee also made it clear that we should never make harsh and cruel judgment of our neighbor, because we are all in need of understanding and mercy from our loving Heavenly Father for our imperfections. Wasn't this exactly what the Savior taught on another occasion when He said, "And why beholdest thou the mote that is in thy brother's eye, but considerest not the beam that is in thine own eye?" (Matthew 7:3).

We need to consider that it is not easy to understand all the circumstances that contribute to someone's attitude or reaction. Appearances can be deceptive and oftentimes do not represent an accurate measurement of someone's heart. Unlike you and me, Christ is capable of clearly seeing all facets of a given situation. Even knowing all our weaknesses as He does, the Savior does not rashly condemn us but continues to work with us compassionately over time, helping us to remove the

beam from our eye. Jesus always looks on the heart and not merely on the appearance (see 1 Samuel 16:7). He Himself declared, "Judge not according to the appearance" (John 7:24).

Now, consider the Savior's wise counsel to the twelve Nephite disciples regarding this question:

"And know ye that ye shall be judges of this people, according to the judgment which I shall give unto you, which shall be just. Therefore, what manner of men ought ye to be? Verily I say unto you, even as I am" (3 Nephi 27:27).

"Therefore I would that ye should be perfect even as I, or your Father who is in heaven is perfect" (3 Nephi 12:48).

Therefore, the Lord fixes judgment upon those who take it upon themselves to judge unrighteously the supposed shortcomings of others. In order to qualify ourselves to make "righteous judgment" (JST, Matthew 7:2), we must strive to become like the Savior and look at the imperfections of individuals compassionately, even through His eyes. Considering we each still have a long way to go to reach perfection, perhaps it would be better to sit at Jesus's feet and plead for mercy for our own imperfections, as did the repentant woman in the Pharisee's house, and not spend so much time and energy fixating on the perceived imperfections of others.

I testify that as we strive to incorporate the Savior's compassionate example into our lives, our capacity to compliment the virtues of our neighbors will increase and our natural instinct to judge their imperfections will decrease. Our communion with God will grow, and certainly our lives will become sweeter, our feelings more tender, and we will find a never-ending source of happiness. We will be known as peacemakers, whose words are as gentle as the dew of a spring morning.

Chapter 2

JOY AND PEACE IN HIM

The Savior spent His life on earth inviting others to come unto Him and find rest (see Matthew 11:28). His compassionate invitation is extended to all of us no matter the circumstances of our life. The lyrics of this beautiful song remind us of the Savior's loving invitation to us:

> *There is peace in Christ*
> *When we learn of Him.*
> *Feel the love He felt for us*
> *When He bore our sins.*
> *Listen to His words.*
> *Let them come alive. . . .*
>
> *He gives us hope*
> *When hope is gone.*
> *He gives us strength*
> *When we can't go on.*
> *He gives us shelter*
> *In the storms of life.*[1]

In 2021, our beloved prophet, President Russell M. Nelson, taught: "For the past year, we have all been dealing with dramatic and unexpected events. Amid such uncertainty, there is only one way to feel at peace. . . . That peace is found in faith in the Lord Jesus Christ."[2]

You may have concerns about how you can feel confidence and peace about the future when the conditions of the world do not look promising. You may find it difficult to feel and share love among all of God's children during times of such contention and unrest. I assure you that your confidence in your Savior Jesus Christ will strengthen you to continue moving forward in life and extending compassion to others despite the challenges you go through.

Coming unto Him does not tie us down or limit our freedom! Rather, it gives us reason for firm hope and provides a solid anchor to our souls, giving us the lasting inner peace and love that we need to live in these days and find rest in Him. If we don't turn away from the light we receive from the Savior, instead of a hollow feeling of emptiness in our lives, we can experience a fullness that occupies the innermost chambers of our souls. It is through the Savior Jesus Christ and His healing, atoning sacrifice that we are enabled to stand tall and strong, even in the face of adversity. The Savior's healing power can fill our souls with peace, light, understanding, joy, and love—even in times of trial.

These trials and tests are part of the plan of happiness of God for all His children, including for those who are trying their best to do everything right. I know that going through trials is not an easy task. Of course, we don't enjoy it. Sometimes our trials can even oppress us to such a point that our spiritual light seems to dim. But it is declared in the scriptures that it is necessary to have opposition in all things (see 2 Nephi 2:11). How could we recognize the sweet without experiencing the bitter? We all can get the strength we need to endure our trials from the Savior and His atoning sacrifice. The Savior descended below all things, so He understands pain and He is aware of our adversities. His heart is full of mercy, and He is always ready to help us in any circumstances. His love and compassion for us are everlasting (see Jeremiah 31:3).

We are living in a very interesting time. We are seeing many tumultuous events in the world. Many of us are still feeling the sobering effects of the COVID-19 pandemic in addition to facing so many other problems of our day. All these circumstances can cause confusion in the minds of people. That confusion causes some to forget who Jesus Christ is and what He did for us. Those in this circumstance will often turn to the philosophies of men for answers, rather than the doctrine of Christ. The enemy of truth and his followers are taking every opportunity to create even more distraction and confusion in our minds and contention in our hearts, relentlessly trying our faith and our self-esteem. These events may generate fear and uncertainty about our future. But we feel the assurance that it is totally possible for each of us to carry out what the Lord has foreordained us to do in these days as we seek and follow Him and walk in His covenant path. I promise you, as an Apostle of Jesus Christ, that as you turn to Him—to His doctrine—in times of doubt, difficulty, and confusion, you will be blessed with the answers and the assurance we all need. These answers will be specific and personal to all of us, individually.

In December of 1832, a group of Saints in the early Church received a personal invitation from the Savior through a revelation given to Joseph Smith. This is what the Lord said: "Draw near unto me and I will draw near unto you; seek me diligently and ye shall find me" (Doctrine and Covenants 88:63). This invitation is extended to all of us in our day. As we commit our faith and energy to draw closer to Jesus Christ, we begin to understand more fully who He really is. We begin to gain a deep and abiding testimony of His matchless love and the blessings of His great atoning sacrifice. We truly begin to find Him and to recognize Him as the Creator of the earth, the Redeemer of all mankind, the Only Begotten of the Father, the King of kings, the Prince of Peace.

The more we draw near unto Him, the more we begin to understand His eternal message of salvation and exaltation. We recognize that He continues to beckon us to come and

follow Him and that His doctrine is perfect and every bit as applicable today as it was throughout all previous generations. And finally, we begin to appreciate more profoundly His role as the Holy Messiah of the world and what occurred in Gethsemane and on Calvary. Although He was convicted and sentenced unfairly, in a supreme act of compassion, He gave His life willingly to fulfill His own prophetic words. This priceless gift brings immortality to all and eternal life to the obedient and faithful.

As we diligently draw near unto the Savior, we will find Him, feel His love for us, and understand more clearly the answers to our prayers. The Psalmist wrote: "Cast thy burden upon the Lord, and he shall sustain thee" (Psalm 55:22). "And then may God grant unto [us] that [our] burdens may be light, through the joy of his Son" (Alma 33:23). One of the great lessons I have learned in my life is to see trials through the eyes of faith. I have learned that healing comes, but in the Lord's time and in His way. Without seeing our trials with the eyes of faith and trusting in the Lord's wisdom, it is difficult to endure in our challenges.

I believe that our experiences can help us to turn our hearts to the Savior and draw nearer to Him and to one another. As we seek Him with all the energy of our hearts, focusing our thoughts, our prayers, our faith, and our desires on

Him, we will receive, by His grace, His influence in our life and will enjoy the blessings of His atoning sacrifice.

Jesus Christ is the source of true peace in this world. Throughout the dispensations, He has repeatedly invited His people to seek Him in every thought and to follow Him with their hearts. The Lord counseled Joseph Smith to "treasure these things up in your hearts, and let the solemnities of eternity rest upon your minds" (Doctrine and Covenants 43:34). In so doing, we align our mind and desires with His. Adopting this path in our life demonstrates that we are striving to conduct our lives in harmony with the gospel of Jesus Christ. It shows that our daily focus is on everything that is good and that we seek to emulate Him.

President Nelson has taught that when we focus our energy on Jesus Christ and His gospel, "we can feel joy regardless of what is happening—or not happening—in our lives." He further explained that joy comes from and because of Christ, and that He is the source of all joy. "For Latter-day Saints, Jesus Christ is joy."[3] As we rely upon the Rock of Salvation, the Savior of our souls, and act in faith on His invitation to come and find rest in Him, we will be strengthened to deal with our struggles, our weaknesses, and our temptations. He will increase our capacity to feel a consistent peace in every circumstance of our lives.

As we contemplate the strength and hope that we can receive from the Savior, we have reason to lift up our heads, rejoice, and press forward in faith without wavering, "for he that wavereth is like a wave of the sea driven with the wind and tossed. . . . A double minded man is unstable in all his ways" (James 1:6, 8).

Listen to the Savior's own words as He entreats us:

"Let not your heart be troubled: ye believe in God, believe also in me. . . . If ye love me, keep my commandments. . . . He that hath my commandments, and keepeth them, he it is that loveth me: and he that loveth me shall be loved of my Father, and I will love him, and will manifest myself to him" (John 14:1, 15, 21).

God is able to bless us according to our faith in Him and in His Son, Jesus Christ, which is the source of living with divine purpose and eternal perspective. Faith is a practical principle that inspires diligence. It is a vital, living force manifested in our positive attitude and desire to willingly do everything that God and Jesus Christ ask of us. Faith can take us to our knees to implore the Lord for guidance and move us to arise and act with confidence to achieve things consistent with His will.

Years ago while serving as a mission president, I received a phone call from the parents of one of our beloved missionaries informing me of the death of his sister. I remember, in the

tenderness of that moment, that missionary and I discussed God's marvelous plan of salvation for His children and how this knowledge would comfort him.

Although he was stunned and saddened by that adversity, this missionary—through his tears and with faith in God—rejoiced in his sister's life. He expressed unwavering confidence in the tender mercies of the Lord. Resolutely, he told me that he would continue to serve his mission with all faith and diligence in order to be worthy of the promises that God had for him and his family. In this time of need, that faithful missionary turned his heart to God, placed all of his trust in Him, and renewed his commitment to serve the Lord. His decision demonstrated a deep and abiding love for his Savior, for his sister, and for the people whom he would invite unto Christ during his mission.

If we are steadfast and do not waver in our faith, the Lord through His love and grace will increase our capacity to raise ourselves above the challenges and heartaches of life. We will be able to overcome temptation, and we will develop the capacity to endure even what appear to be overwhelming obstacles and sorrows.

All of us can receive the strength to choose the right if we seek the Lord and place all our trust and faith in Him. But, as the scriptures teach, we need to have "a sincere heart" and "real intent." Then the Lord, in His infinite mercy, "will manifest the truth . . . unto [us], by the power of the Holy Ghost. And by the power of the Holy Ghost [we] may know the truth of all things" (Moroni 10:4–5).

This knowledge acquired through the Holy Ghost is our testimony, which propels our faith and determination to follow the teachings of the restored gospel in these latter days, regardless of the popular messages we hear from the world. Our testimony must be our shield to protect us against the fiery darts of the adversary in his attempts to attack us. It will guide us safely through the darkness and confusion that exist in the world today.

I learned this principle when I served as a young missionary. My companion and I were serving in a very remote branch of the Church. We tried to speak with every person in the city. They received us very well, but they liked to debate the scriptures and asked us for concrete evidence regarding the truthfulness of what we were teaching.

I recall that each time my companion and I set out to try to prove something to people in a debate, the Spirit of God left us, and we felt totally lost and confused. We soon felt that we should more strongly align our testimonies with the truths of the gospel we were teaching. From that time on, when we bore a testimony with all our hearts, speaking with sincere compassion for those we were teaching, a silent, confirming power would come from the Holy Ghost. It filled the room and there was no space for confusion or debate. From those experiences on my mission, I learned the power of a sincere and loving testimony of a true disciple of Jesus Christ.

The Savior Himself taught that the adversary desires to sift us as wheat, causing us to lose our ability to influence the world for good (see Luke 22:31–32). Because of the wave of confusion and doubt spreading throughout the world today, we must hold ever more tightly to our testimony of the gospel of Jesus Christ. Then will our ability to defend truth and justice greatly increase. We will feel peace and joy in His love. We will win the daily battles against evil, and, rather than fall on the battlefields of life, we will rally others to the Master's standards.

I invite all to find safety in the teachings contained in the scriptures. They are a blessing from our loving Father in Heaven to help guide us in our day. I invite all to find safety in the wise words of our current prophets. They too are an evidence of the Savior's compassion for us, sharing His will for our lives and providing us with comfort and counsel. I invite all to trust in the merits and in the power of the Atonement of Jesus Christ. Through His atoning sacrifice, this supreme act of love, we can gain the courage to win all the battles of our time, even in the midst of our difficulties, challenges, and temptations.

Let us trust in His love and power to save us. Christ Himself said:

"I am the way, the truth, and the life: no man cometh unto the Father, but by me" (John 14:6).

"I am the light of the world: he that followeth me shall not walk in darkness, but shall have the light of life" (John 8:12).

"These things I have spoken unto you, that in me ye might have peace. In the world ye shall have tribulation: but be of good cheer; I have overcome the world" (John 16:33).

Place your trust in God and in the teachings of His prophets. Renew your covenants with God, to serve and love Him with all your heart, regardless of the complex situations of life. By the power of your unwavering faith in Christ, you will become free of the captivity of sin, of doubt, of unbelief, of unhappiness, of suffering, and of contention, and you will receive all of the blessings our loving Heavenly Father has promised.

God is real. He lives. He loves us. He listens to our prayers in our moments of happiness and in our moments of doubt, sadness, and desperation. Jesus Christ is the Savior of the world. He is the Redeemer. I find evidence of Their love for us and take comfort in the lyrics of the hymn "Not Now, but in the Coming Years," found in the Portuguese hymnal:

> *If clouds instead of sun spread shadows o'er our heart,*
> *If pain afflicts us, never mind; we will soon know who*
>   *Thou art.*

Jesus guides us with His hand, and He will tell us why;
If we listen to His voice, He will tell us by and by.
Confide in God unwaveringly, and let Him us sustain;
Sing His glory endlessly, for later He'll explain.[4]

Chapter 3

BEING MEEK AND LOWLY OF HEART

Mormon taught that a person "cannot have faith and hope, save he shall be meek, and lowly of heart" (Moroni 7:43). He added that without such attributes, "faith and hope is vain, for none is acceptable before God, save the meek and lowly in heart" (v. 44).

Meekness is the quality of those who are "Godfearing, righteous, humble, teachable, and patient under suffering."[1] Those who possess this Christlike attribute are willing to follow Jesus Christ. They are submissive to God, and their temperament is calm, docile, and patient. Meekness allows us to see our own weaknesses and be compassionate toward others' weaknesses. At the core of any Christlike charity toward our neighbor is humility.

The Apostle Paul taught that meekness is a fruit of the Spirit (see Galatians 5:23). Therefore, it can most easily be attained if we "live in the Spirit" (v. 25). And to live in the Spirit, our lifestyle must reflect righteousness before the Lord.

As we take Christ's name upon us, it is expected that we strive to emulate His attributes and change our character to become more like Him each day. The Savior, admonishing His disciples, said, "Be ye therefore perfect, even as your Father which is in heaven is perfect" (Matthew 5:48). If we "come unto Christ, . . . deny [ourselves] of all ungodliness; . . . and love God," then through Christ's grace the day will come when we may be perfect in Him (Moroni 10:32).

"Christlike attributes are gifts from God. [These attributes] come as [we] use [our] agency righteously. . . . With a desire to please God, [we have to] recognize [our] weaknesses and be willing and anxious to improve."[2]

Meekness is vital for us to become more Christlike. Without it we won't be able to develop other important virtues. Being meek does not mean being weak; rather, it means behaving with goodness and kindness, showing strength, serenity, healthy self-worth, and self-control.

Meekness was one of the most abundant attributes in the Savior's life. He taught His disciples, "Learn of me; for I am meek and lowly in heart" (Matthew 11:29).

We are blessed to be born with the seed of meekness in our hearts as part of our divine nature as children of our Heavenly Father. We need to understand that it is not possible to grow and develop that seed in the twinkling of an eye but rather over time. Christ asks us to "take up [our] cross daily" (Luke 9:23), meaning that it must be a constant focus and desire.

President Lorenzo Snow, the fifth prophet of our dispensation, taught, "It is our duty to try to be perfect, . . . to improve each day, and look upon our course last week and do things better this week; do things better today than we did them yesterday."[3] So one of the steps of becoming meek is to improve day by day. Each day we need to try to be better than the previous.

President Snow added:

> We have our little follies and our weaknesses; we should try to overcome them as fast as possible, and . . . should [instill] this feeling in the hearts of our children . . . that they may learn to [behave] properly before Him under all circumstances.
>
> If the husband can live with his wife one day without quarrelling or without treating anyone unkindly or without grieving the Spirit of God . . . he is so far perfect. Then let him try to be the same the next day. But supposing he should fail in this his next day's attempt, that is no reason why he should not succeed in doing so the third day.[4]

Upon acknowledging our dedication and perseverance, the Lord will give us that which we are not able to attain due to our imperfections and human weaknesses. Though we are not perfect, the Lord in His loving compassion will help us to become perfected in Him.

An important step to becoming meek is learning how to control our temper. Because the natural man dwells within each one of us and because we live in a world full of pressure, controlling our temper can be a great challenge for some. Think for a few seconds how you react when someone does not comply with your desires the moment you want them to. What about when people disagree with your ideas, even though you are "absolutely sure" that your ideas represent the proper solution to a problem? What is your response when someone offends you, critiques your efforts, or is simply unkind because he or she is in a bad mood? At these moments and in other difficult situations, we must learn to control our temper and convey our feelings with patience and gentle persuasion. This is most important within our home and in our relationship with our spouse. During the four decades and counting that I've been married to my sweetheart, she has given me gentle reminders of this as we have faced life's unsettling challenges.

Among instructions found in his Second Epistle to Timothy, the Apostle Paul said: "And the servant of the Lord must not strive; but be gentle unto all men, apt to teach, patient, in meekness instructing those that oppose themselves; if God peradventure will give them repentance to the

acknowledging of the truth; and that they may recover themselves" (2 Timothy 2:24–26).

By controlling our reactions, being calm and temperate, and avoiding contention, we will begin to qualify for the gift of meekness. President Henry B. Eyring once said, "When we with faith control our tempers and subdue our pride, the Holy Ghost gives His approval, and sacred promises and covenants become sure."[5]

Another step to attain meekness is to become humble. The Lord instructed Thomas B. Marsh through the Prophet Joseph Smith, saying, "Be thou humble; and the Lord thy God shall lead thee by the hand, and give thee answer to thy prayers" (Doctrine and Covenants 112:10).

I believe that only those who are humble are able to acknowledge and understand the Lord's answers to their prayers. The humble are teachable, recognizing how dependent they are on God and desiring to be subject to His will. The humble and meek have the ability to influence others to be the same. God's promise to the humble is that He will lead them by the hand. I truly believe that we can avoid potential detours and much sadness in our lives as we walk hand in hand with the Lord.

One of the most beautiful modern-day examples of meekness that I am aware of is that of Brother Moses Mahlangu. His conversion began in 1964, when he received a copy of the Book of Mormon. He was fascinated as he read this book, but it was not until the early '70s that he saw a sign for The Church of Jesus Christ of Latter-day Saints on a building in Johannesburg, South Africa, as he was walking down a street. Brother Mahlangu was intrigued and entered the building to learn more about the Church. He was kindly told that he could not attend the services or be baptized because the country's laws did not allow it at that time.

Brother Mahlangu accepted that difficult news with meekness, humility, and without resentment, and he continued to have a strong desire to learn more about the Church. He asked the Church leaders if they could leave one of the meetinghouse windows open during the Sunday meetings so he could sit outside and listen to the services. For several years, Brother Mahlangu's family and friends attended church regularly "through the window." One day in 1980, they were told that they could attend church and also be baptized. What a glorious day it was for Brother Mahlangu.

Later the Church organized a branch in his neighborhood in Soweto. This was possible only because of the determination, courage, and faithfulness of people like Brother Mahlangu who remained faithful for so many years under difficult circumstances.

One of Brother Mahlangu's friends, who had joined the Church at the same time, was the one who recounted this story to me when I visited the Soweto stake. At the end of our

conversation, he gave me a hug. At that moment, I felt as if I were encircled in the Savior's loving arms. Meekness emanated from this good brother's eyes. With a heart full of goodness and deep gratitude, he asked if I could tell our prophet how grateful and blessed he and many others were for having the true gospel in their lives. Brother Mahlangu and his friend's example of meekness truly influenced many lives for good—especially mine.

The Savior Jesus Christ is the supreme example of meekness. Even during the last moments of His mortal life, after being unfairly accused and condemned, painfully carrying His cross toward Golgotha, being mocked and cursed by His enemies, and being abandoned by many who knew Him and had witnessed His miracles, He allowed Himself to be nailed to the cross. Christ faced extreme physical and spiritual suffering, giving us the opportunity to change our spiritual character and become meek like Him.

Jesus Christ is our Savior. Thanks to His love, it is possible to change. It is possible to leave our weaknesses behind. It is possible to reject the evil influences in our lives, control our anger, become meek, and develop the attributes of our Savior. He showed us the way. He gave us the perfect example and commanded each one of us to become as He is. His invitation to us is to follow Him, follow His example, and become like Him.

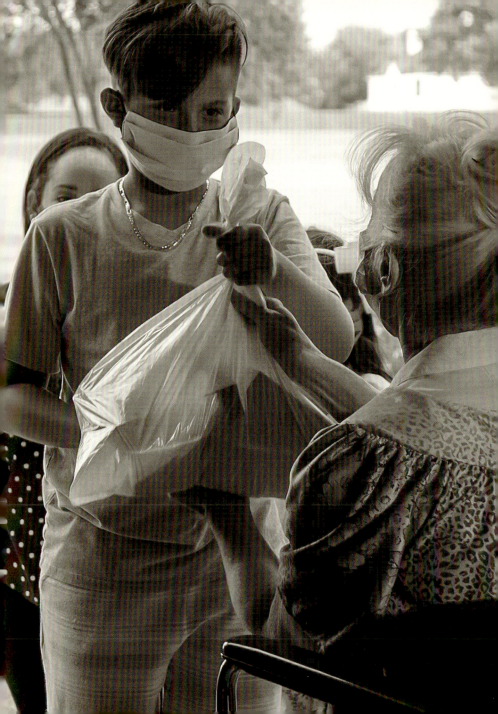

Chapter 4

MINISTERING TO ALL

On one occasion the Savior asked a question to Peter three times: "Simon, son of Jonas, lovest thou me? He saith unto him, Yea, Lord; thou knowest that I love thee. [Jesus] saith unto him, Feed my sheep" (John 21:16).

Because He was deeply concerned with the welfare of our Heavenly Father's children, the Lord gave Peter the special charge of feeding His sheep.

He reaffirmed this same concern in modern times through a revelation given to Joseph Smith: "Now, I say unto you, and what I say unto you, I say unto all the Twelve: Arise and gird up your loins, take up your cross, follow me, and feed my sheep" (Doctrine and Covenants 112:14).

As we study the scriptures, we notice that the Savior ministered to people according to their specific needs. A good example of this occurred when He was near Capernaum, and Jairus, a ruler of the synagogue, fell down at Jesus's feet and pleaded with the Lord to come into his house and bless his daughter, who was dying. Jesus went with Jairus even though the crowd made it difficult for Him to move fast.

And then a messenger came, telling Jairus his daughter was already dead. Even grieving as he was, Jairus kept his steadfast faith in the Lord, who comforted the heart of that father, saying: "Fear not: believe only, and she shall be made whole. And when he came into the house, he suffered no man to go in, save Peter, and James, and John, and the father and the mother of the maiden. And all wept, and bewailed her: but he said, Weep not; she is not dead, but sleepeth. . . . And he . . . took her by the hand, and called, saying, Maid, arise. And her spirit came again, and she arose straightway: and he commanded to give her meat" (Luke 8:50–52, 54–55).

Jesus showed patience and love to all who came to Him seeking relief for their physical, emotional, or spiritual illnesses and who felt discouraged and downtrodden.

To follow the Savior's example, each one of us must look around and reach out to the sheep who are facing the same circumstances and lift them up and encourage them to proceed on the journey toward eternal life. This need today is as great as or perhaps even greater than when the Savior walked on this earth. As shepherds, we must understand that we should nurture each one of our sheep to bring them to Christ, which is the purpose of all that we do in this Church.

Any activity, meeting, or program should focus on this same objective. As we stay in tune with the needs of the people, we can strengthen them and help them overcome their challenges so they will remain steadfast in the way that will lead them back to our Heavenly Father's presence and help them endure to the end.

The gospel of Jesus Christ is about people, not programs. Sometimes, in the haste of fulfilling our Church responsibilities, we spend too much time concentrating on programs instead of focusing on people, and we end up overlooking their real needs. When that happens, we may lose the perspective of our callings, neglect people, and fail to truly help others attain their divine potential to gain eternal life.

Let me illustrate this with an example from my own life. As I was about to have my twelfth birthday, my bishop invited me in for an interview and taught me how to prepare to receive the Aaronic Priesthood and be ordained a deacon. As the interview was coming to an end, he pulled out a set of forms from his desk and challenged me to fill them out. They were mission call papers. I was astonished. After all, I was only eleven. But that bishop had a vision of the future and of the blessings that would be mine if I prepared properly to serve a mission when my time came.

He showed he really cared about me. He told me the steps I should take to prepare both spiritually and financially to serve the Lord. After that day, he, and then the bishop who was called after him, interviewed me at least twice a year until I was nineteen and encouraged me to remain faithful in my preparation.

They kept my missionary forms in my file and mentioned them whenever we had an interview. With my parents' help and with the encouragement of loving and patient bishops, I served a mission. That mission helped me gain a perspective of the blessings God has in store for all who endure to the end.

It does not matter whether it is a child, youth, or adult—everyone needs to feel loved. We have been counseled for several years to focus on working with new converts and less-active members. People are much more likely to remain in the Church when they feel someone cares for them.

Among the last instructions the Savior gave His Apostles, He said: "A new commandment I give unto you, That ye love one another; as I have loved you, that ye also love one another. By this shall all men know that ye are my disciples, if ye have love one to another" (John 13:34–35).

People are most receptive to our influence when they feel that we truly love them, and not only because we have a calling to fulfill. As we express true love for people, they will be able to feel the influence of the Spirit and may feel motivated to follow our teachings.

It is not always easy to love people exactly as they are. The prophet Mormon explained what we should do if such challenges arise: "Wherefore, my beloved brethren, pray unto the Father with all the energy of heart, that ye may be filled with this love, which he hath bestowed upon all who are true followers of his Son, Jesus Christ; that ye may become the sons of God; that when he shall appear we shall be like him, for we shall see him as he is; that we may have this hope; that we may be purified even as he is pure" (Moroni 7:48).

Christ Himself ministered to people, lifting the heavy-laden, giving hope to the disheartened, and seeking after the ones who were lost. He showed people how much He loved and understood them and how precious they were. He acknowledged their divine nature and eternal value. Even when calling people to repentance, He focused on condemning the sin rather than condemning the sinner.

In his First Epistle to the Corinthians, the Apostle Paul emphasized the need to express this true love to each sheep of the Lord's flock: "And though I bestow all my goods to feed the poor, and though I give my body to be burned, and have not charity, it profiteth me nothing. Charity suffereth long, and is kind; charity envieth not; charity vaunteth not itself, is not puffed up, doth not behave itself unseemly, seeketh not her own, is not easily provoked, thinketh no evil; rejoiceth not in iniquity, but rejoiceth in the truth; beareth all things, believeth all things, hopeth all things, endureth all things. . . . And now abideth faith, hope, charity, these three; but the greatest of these is charity" (1 Corinthians 13:3–7, 13).

As we follow the Savior's example and teachings, we can assist people to fulfill their earthly mission that they might return to live with our Heavenly Father.

An essential aspect of truly ministering to those around us is becoming one with them. The Lord has said, "If ye are not one ye are not mine" (Doctrine and Covenants 38:27). In all things we must strive to knit our hearts together in unity and love (see Mosiah 18:21).

My home country of Brazil is very rich in natural resources. One of these resources is the famous Amazon River, one of the largest and longest rivers in the world. It is formed by two separate rivers, the Solimões and Negro. Interestingly, they flow together for a number of miles as the Amazon River before the waters blend, due to the rivers having very different origins, speeds, temperatures, and chemical compositions. After several miles, the waters finally blend together, becoming a different river than its individual parts. The Amazon River becomes so powerful that when it reaches the Atlantic Ocean, it pushes back the seawater so far that fresh water can still be found for many miles out into the ocean.

In a similar way that the Solimões and Negro Rivers flow together to make the great Amazon River, the children of God come together in the restored Church of Jesus Christ from different social backgrounds, traditions, and cultures, forming this wonderful community of Saints in Christ. Eventually, as we encourage, support, and love each other, we combine to form a mighty force for good in the world. As followers of Jesus Christ, flowing as one in this river of goodness, we will be able to provide the "fresh water" of the gospel to a thirsty world.

The Lord has inspired His prophets to teach us how we can support and love each other so we can become united in faith and purpose in following Jesus Christ. Paul, the New Testament Apostle, taught that those who "have been baptized into Christ have put on Christ . . . : for ye are all *one in Christ Jesus*" (Galatians 3:27–28; emphasis added).

When we promise at baptism to follow the Savior, we witness before the Father that we are willing to take upon us the name of Christ. As we strive to acquire His divine attributes in our lives, we become different than we were, through the Atonement of Christ the Lord, and our love for all people increases naturally. We feel a sincere concern for everyone's welfare and happiness. We see each other as brothers and sisters—as children of God with divine origin, attributes, and potential. We desire to care for each other and bear one another's burdens (see Mosiah 18:8).

This is what Paul described as charity (see 1 Corinthians 13). Mormon, a prophet of the Book of Mormon, described it as "the pure love of Christ" (Moroni 7:47), which is the most sublime, noblest, and strongest form of love. A modern-day prophet, President Russell M. Nelson, described a manifestation of this pure love of Christ as ministering, which is a more focused and holier approach to love and care for other individuals like the Savior did.[1]

Let us consider this principle of love and care, as the Savior did, within the context of encouraging, helping, and supporting those who are recent converts and those beginning to show interest in attending our Church services.

When these new friends come out of the world and embrace the gospel of Jesus Christ, joining His Church, they become His disciples, being born again through Him (see Mosiah 27:25). They leave behind a world they knew well and choose to follow Jesus Christ, with full purpose of heart, joining a new "river" like the mighty Amazon River—a river that is a valiant force of goodness and righteousness that flows toward the presence of God. The Apostle Peter describes it as "a chosen generation, a royal priesthood, an holy nation, a peculiar people" (1 Peter 2:9). As these new friends merge into this new and unfamiliar river, they may feel a little lost at first. They find themselves blending into a river with unique origins, temperatures, and chemical compositions—a river that

has its own traditions, culture, and vocabulary. This new life in Christ may seem overwhelming for them. Think for a moment about how they may feel as they hear for the first time such expressions as "fast Sunday," "baptism for the dead," "triple combination," and so forth.

It is easy to see why they may feel like they don't belong. In such situations, they may ask themselves, "Is there a place for me here? Do I fit into The Church of Jesus Christ of Latter-day Saints? Does the Church need me? Will I find new friends willing to help and support me?"

In such moments, those of us who are at different points in the long journey of discipleship must extend a warm hand of fellowship to our new friends, accept them where they are, and help, love, and include them. All of these new friends are precious sons and daughters of God. We cannot afford to lose even one of them, because, like the Amazon River that depends on tributaries feeding it, we need them just as much as they need us, to become a mighty force for good in the world.

Our new friends bring God-given talents, excitement, and goodness within them. Their enthusiasm for the gospel can be contagious, thereby helping us revitalize our own testimonies. They also bring fresh perspectives to our understanding of life and the gospel.

We have long been taught how we can help our new friends to feel welcome and loved in the restored Church of Jesus Christ. They need three things so they may remain strong and faithful throughout their lives:

First, they need brothers and sisters in the Church who are sincerely interested in them, true and loyal friends to whom they can constantly turn, who will walk beside them, and who will answer their questions. As members, we should always be attentive and look for new faces when attending Church activities and meetings, regardless of the responsibilities, assignments, or concerns we may have. We can do simple things to help these new friends feel embraced and welcome in the Church, such as giving a warm greeting, smiling sincerely at them, sitting together to sing and worship, introducing them to other members, and so forth. As we open our hearts to our new friends in some of these ways, we are acting in the spirit of ministering. When we minister to them like the Savior did, they won't feel like "strangers within our gates." They will feel like they can fit in and make new friends, and most importantly, they will feel the Savior's love through our genuine care.

Second, new friends need an assignment—an opportunity to serve others. Service is one of the greatest aspects of The Church of Jesus Christ of Latter-day Saints. It is a process by which our faith can grow stronger. Every new friend deserves that opportunity. While the bishop and ward council have direct responsibility to extend assignments soon after a baptism, nothing prevents us, as members, from inviting our new

friends to help us serve others informally or through service projects.

Third, new friends must be "nourished by the good word of God" (Moroni 6:4). We can help them to love and become familiar with the scriptures as we read and discuss their teachings with them, providing context to the stories and explaining difficult words. We can also teach them how to receive personal guidance through regular scripture study. In addition, we can reach out to our new friends in their own homes and invite them to ours at times outside of our regularly scheduled Church meetings and activities, helping them merge into the mighty river of the community of Saints.

Recognizing the adjustments and challenges our new friends make in becoming members of God's family, as their brothers and sisters, we can share how we have overcome similar challenges in our lives. This will help them know that they are not alone and that God will bless them as they exercise faith in His promises.

When the Solimões and Negro Rivers blend together, the Amazon River becomes mighty and strong. In a similar fashion, when we and our new friends truly merge, the restored Church of Jesus Christ becomes even stronger and steadier. My sweetheart, Rosana, and I are so grateful for all those who helped us to blend into this new river many years ago, when we each embraced the gospel of Jesus Christ in our home country of Brazil. Throughout the years, these wonderful people have truly ministered to us and have helped us to continue flowing in righteousness. We are so grateful for them.

Early prophets in the Western Hemisphere knew well how to keep new friends flowing faithfully together into this new river of goodness toward eternal life. For example, having seen our day and knowing that we would face similar challenges, Moroni included some of those important steps in his writings in the Book of Mormon:

"And after they had been received unto baptism, and were wrought upon and cleansed by the power of the Holy Ghost, they were numbered among the people of the church of Christ; and their names were taken, that they might be remembered and nourished by the good word of God, to keep them in the right way, to keep them continually watchful unto prayer, relying alone upon the merits of Christ, who was the author and the finisher of their faith. And the church did meet together oft, to fast and to pray, and to speak one with another concerning the welfare of their souls" (Moroni 6:4–5).

I believe we can do much better and should do better in welcoming new friends into the Church. I invite you to consider what we can do to be more embracing, accepting, and helpful to them, starting this very next Sunday. Be careful not to let the checklist of duties for your Church assignments get in the way of welcoming new friends at meetings and activities.

After all, these souls are precious before the eyes of God and are much more important than programs and activities. If we minister to our new friends with our hearts full of pure love as the Savior did, I promise you, in His name, that He will assist us in our efforts. When we act as faithful ministers, as the Savior did, our new friends will have the help they need to remain strong, dedicated, and faithful to the end. They will join us as we become a mighty people of God and will help us to bring fresh water to a world desperately in need of the blessings of the gospel of Jesus Christ. These children of God will feel like they are "no more strangers and foreigners, but fellowcitizens with the saints" (Ephesians 2:19). They will recognize the presence of our Savior, Jesus Christ, in His own Church. They will continue to flow with us as a river into the fountain of all goodness until they are received with open arms by our Lord, Jesus Christ, and they hear the Father say, "Ye *shall* have eternal life" (2 Nephi 31:20; emphasis added).

Seek the Lord's help in loving others as He has loved you. Let us all follow the counsel given by Mormon: "Wherefore, my beloved brethren [and sisters], pray unto the Father with all the energy of heart, that ye may be filled with this love, which he hath bestowed upon all who are true followers of his Son, Jesus Christ" (Moroni 7:48).

Chapter 5

LOVING THOSE WHO ARE DIFFERENT FROM US

As we strive to become good disciples of Jesus Christ, we should be more intentional in our efforts to be good ministers. We should understand and have empathy for every person. This is part of developing Christlike compassion.

My parents were baptized into The Church of Jesus Christ of Latter-day Saints when I was a little boy. They were already good people before becoming members of the Church, but they of course had some worldly habits. My father used to drink and smoke and had other habits that had come from the world. My mother was a very religious person, but she also had a different lifestyle from what is practiced by members of the Church. What really helped them to stay in the restored Church of Jesus Christ was the group of people in our little branch that embraced us, helped us, and loved us. We would receive visits every other week from someone in the Church. We would often be invited to home evenings in their homes. They did everything possible to bring us together in that new environment. I believe my parents stayed in the Church because of these people who were good disciples of Jesus Christ and who reached out in their Christlike love to them.

When we understand people and their conditions and circumstances, we tend to act in love toward them. We tend to embrace them according to their needs. We should strive always to minister to people according to the circumstances in which they are living. To do this as the Savior would, we have to understand their challenges and their difficulties.

We appreciate the diversity in culture, ethnicity, and language that exists among us. They are gifts to the human family. We may be raised in different countries and environments with different cultures and ways of thinking. But we should not forget that we are all brothers and sisters; we are all children of the same Father in Heaven; we are more alike than different. Indeed, we, being many and different, are one, are we not?

While we may be different in some respects, there is a unity that each of us can nurture now. We are "one" in the quest to return to a heavenly home we once knew. We are "one" in our imperfect state. We are "one" in that we each have spiritual gifts. We are "one" and each has the capacity to grow, whatever our circumstances. We are "one," are we not? By a common spiritual measure, each of us is as valuable as the person next to us because of a just and merciful Savior, a value that surpasses any earthly valuation. Therefore, our love for others should transcend our differences in culture, ethnicity, or language. We should be patient with others; we should show love and respect for all.

As children of God we come from the same spiritual root. Even though we were put here on this earth in different circumstances, we should not blame or ridicule one another because of that. Our different circumstances of life can be a unique experience to grow. We can learn from different people's point of view. As we live with our differences and try to learn from them and improve ourselves, we become more understanding and more like our Savior.

One of the strongest powers in the world is the power of the pure love of Christ, which is charity (see Moroni 7:47). Charity is a Christlike attribute. As we charitably give of ourselves to people, they can feel this type of love that the Savior has for them. We all can be an instrument in His hands in that regard. Service and compassion are not about us—not about me or about you. They are about what the Savior, Jesus Christ, wants to accomplish through us. That is why the Lord gives us the opportunity to serve. We are called to help people to feel the Savior's love.

My family and I have experienced the feelings of comfort and peace that Christlike ministering can bring on several different occasions. On a cold and rainy weekend in 2002, my family and I traveled on ecclesiastical assignment to a faraway Church branch. Our three children were then six, ten, and thirteen years old. When we had traveled for several hours, we decided to stop in a picturesque town to get out of the car for a few minutes and stretch our legs before completing our journey. We decided to explore the town a little during that stop and learned that they were holding a traditional local festival. Due to the festival, the little city was packed with visitors and locals. The scheduled events were taking place around one of the local churches near the center of town. Around the church, there were many vendors selling typical foods and local handicrafts. After walking for a while, two of my children and I returned to the car, but my wife and our ten-year-old daughter continued looking at the vendors' goods for a little longer.

Among these vendors there were also many people begging, and it was those poverty-stricken people who caught my daughter's attention. She had seen people begging before, but perhaps not in such numbers. Two of them in particular caught her attention: a man who was missing a leg, and at his side, a little girl, about seven years old. They were wet from the rain, and the girl, who didn't have a coat, was shivering from the cold. My daughter, moved by compassion, didn't hesitate to take off her very nice coat—the only one she had brought on the trip—and give it to the cold little girl. My wife and daughter then returned to the car without saying a word about

what had happened. None of us who were already in the car noticed that my daughter had come back without her coat, and we continued our trip until we reached the city where the little branch was. The next day was Sunday, and as we left the hotel to go to church, I told my daughter to put her coat on because it was very cold outside. Instead of going to put her coat on as I had instructed, she simply went to the car. Only then did my wife recount what had happened the day before.

Feelings of compassion are often awakened in times of great need. But when these feelings are awakened, it is because they are already within us; it is because of the divinity that exists within us, children of Heavenly Father, who is the ultimate giver of compassion. President Marion G. Romney taught, "The truth is, my beloved brethren and sisters, man is a child of God—a God in embryo."[1] These feelings of compassion are engrained in our very spiritual makeup, but we don't always use our free will in the way that motivates action for good. Our daughter had already been taught about charity and other principles of the gospel. On that day, she actively experienced, for herself, this godly attribute. Upon seeing a young girl in great need, she had a choice. She could have chosen to look in another direction, or she could have done as she did and risen to the occasion. When we utilize these divine attributes by our faithful actions and not solely in empty and trite words, the word *compassion* will be engraved in our mind and heart, a delightful and desirable mark that will remain in us forever. This mark on our heart will be one of the attributes that truly identifies us as divine offspring of our compassionate and loving Heavenly Father. We read in 1 John 3:2, "And it doth not yet appear what we shall be: but we know that, when he shall appear, we shall be like him." During this mortal sojourn, when an experience evokes this attribute, innate and godlike inclinations within us are awakened; we desire to do good. It is in everyday life that we learn and share lessons of divine love and compassion that last within us. These moments are the true training for eternal life.

Some may wonder how to help close friends who are also members of the Church more fully live the gospel, especially those who might be slipping away. How may we better learn understanding and compassion toward those with whom we do not agree?

Jesus has asked us to observe the law of perfect love, which is a universal gift. He invited us to follow Him, and His invitation to follow Him is an invitation to become like Him. Think of the instance when Jesus was in the house of Simon the Pharisee. Do you remember that occasion—when a woman anointed Jesus's feet and He forgave her sins? Remember what the Lord said about her? In Luke 7:47, the Lord said this: "Wherefore I say unto thee, her sins, which are many, are forgiven; for she loved much: but to whom little is forgiven, the same loveth little." Beautiful, isn't it? Note here that the Savior extended His perfect love to this woman, who was known by everyone around her as a sinner, and how much love she showed Him in return (see 1 John 4:19). So, that's the answer from the Savior for the question of how we interact with those who are very different from us: show a genuine love for them. Try to be a good influence for them through your light, and serve them the best way you can. Let them know you care about them.

We have to remember that our reason for loving other people is not because they are members of the Church or because they are doing the right things. We love them because they are children of God. When Jesus said, "Love one another," He didn't say to love only those that are similar to you, but everyone (see John 13:34–35).

What are we to do when our loved ones have hurt us? How do we forgive their past mistakes and sins and love them anyway?

We learn through the scriptures what the Savior taught about forgiving—that we are required to forgive all men (see Doctrine and Covenants 64:9–10). There is no question about it. But we know that nobody is perfect, and we are all dealing with our own weaknesses, including, sometimes, difficulty in forgiving. Let us explore one aspect of how harmful it is for us

to not forgive. We may better understand how to apply this principle in life when we focus on that side of this question.

When we choose to not forgive others, we become chained by bitterness and anger. This is a heavy burden on us, and it may cause us to lose the influence of the Spirit in our lives. We cannot repent for the mistakes other people make, but we can forgive them. In so doing, we can free ourselves of being someone's judge. We surrender to the Lord, and we stop carrying this heavy burden ourselves. Nurturing negative feelings in our hearts is a roadblock to healing, and, ultimately, to happiness. If we let these feelings go, the Savior can heal our hearts and can help us feel joy once again.

Remember that forgiving others can be an expression of our faith and testimony of the Savior and of the opportunity for forgiveness that He has extended to all of God's children through His atoning sacrifice. The Savior gave His life to separate us from our sins, giving us the power to turn away from our iniquities (see 3 Nephi 20:26). In Moroni 10:8, it is recorded that we should not deny "the gifts of God." When we choose not to forgive, in a sense, we are denying one of the most precious gifts of God—the gift of the Savior's Atonement.

As we strive to be good disciples of Jesus Christ, our character may be tested. We will likely receive criticism no matter our circumstances. Think about the great heroes of the scriptures. They became valiant disciples of the Lord. Peter, for example, moved from being a fisherman to a real rock of the gospel. His example still lives in our hearts. Our strength as an individual depends on how we respond to the tests of life.

Let's live our life with real and focused intent. This is an important character trait for the great achievers in life. They keep persisting in the right direction, no matter the pressure or circumstance or distraction. Our testimony and faith in God and in His Son, Jesus Christ, and in His atoning sacrifice, are the foundation we need to build our lives upon. These are among the greatest powers available to us in this life. President Nelson taught: "Through your faith, Jesus Christ will increase your ability to move the mountains in your life . . . not the mountains of rock that beautify the earth but the mountains of misery in your lives."[2]

Let us always remember that "the worth of souls is great in the sight of God" (Doctrine and Covenants 18:10), and each person you encounter in this life is a beloved son or daughter of heavenly parents. Though we are all different, "all are alike unto God" (2 Nephi 26:33), and as followers of Christ, it is our duty to extend His love to all of God's children.

Chapter 6

ALWAYS REMEMBER HIM

We are living in a very significant time in world history when we are preparing for the Second Coming of Jesus Christ. President Russell M. Nelson once taught, referring to the youth of the Church: "Our Heavenly Father has reserved many of His most noble spirits—perhaps, I might say, His finest team—for this final phase. Those noble spirits—those finest players, those heroes—are *you!* . . . You are among the best the Lord has *ever* sent to this world."[1]

And Sister Nelson said: "There has *never* been a time like this in the history of this world. Never!"[2]

Truly there has never been a time like this in the history of this world! We are living in a time of significant technological, medical, and scientific advancement. Information is available to everyone. Not long ago, when I was a young man, we didn't have any of these powerful tools that are available today that allow us to communicate and obtain information so quickly. This is a great time to be alive.

However, we are also living in challenging times that have been prophesied for centuries by prophets and apostles, both ancient and modern. Throughout history they have expressed their concerns about the last days. We have seen steadily declining moral values that have dramatically changed the world through the years. Modern communication has drawn people into the world and its values, and secularism has changed the way people see God's hand in their lives. As a result, we witness an increasing number of people who are confused about their identity as children of our Heavenly Father. They also have become confused about what really matters in life, and many who were once strong in faith have developed spiritual apathy. How can we continually feel the love of a compassionate Savior and stay firm in our faith in Him despite so many obstacles? Fortunately, our Savior has given us many ways to help God's children feel His love and recognize His sacrifice for them—to see His arms of compassion reaching out to them. One of these is a straightforward invitation from the Doctrine and Covenants that we are reminded of each time we partake of the sacrament: "Always remember him" (Doctrine and Covenants 20:77, 79).

We learn in the scriptures about the cycle of prosperity and pride that has affected God's children throughout human history. In simple words, it is very clear that when people remembered the Lord, they prospered. But when they forgot

Him, they fell into this cycle of pride because of their riches, technological advances, and educational opportunities. As a result, they became a people who rejected the Lord and His covenants and who forgot the poor, the needy, and the strangers around them. Eventually their society collapsed because they became morally bankrupt. Then, through the resulting trials, they became humble, repented, and turned back to the Lord. This same cycle has occurred throughout history among many powerful nations and empires.

I once was reading about Uzziah—or Azariah—one of the kings of Judah, who lived from 792 to 740 BC.[3] His name in Hebrew, *Uziyah,* means "Jehovah is my strength" or "Jehovah's strength."

His life relates to what I just mentioned. At first, Uzziah was known as someone who always remembered the Lord in his life. Even his own name helped him remember the Lord. Uzziah began his reign by seeking, listening to, and worshipping the Lord. The Bible states: "And he [Uzziah] did that which was right in the sight of the Lord. . . . And he sought God in the days of Zechariah, who had understanding in the visions of God: and as long as he sought the Lord, God made him to prosper" (2 Chronicles 26:4–5).

It was during the reign of Uzziah that the kingdom of Judah experienced the greatest period of prosperity and influence since the reign of King Solomon. But unfortunately, pride in his military triumphs and in his great power and wealth caused him to forget the Lord. Because of this sin, Uzziah was struck with leprosy, which forced Uzziah to live isolated from his people until he died (see 2 Kings 15:5; 2 Chronicles 26:21–23).

Uzziah prospered in every way in his life while he remembered the Lord, but when he forgot Him, Uzziah experienced heartbreak, disappointment, and sorrow for his sin.

Based on what happened to Uzziah, how can those who have received so many promises avoid the cycle of prosperity and pride and instead live always in love and humility? How can we avoid being affected by modern-day leprosies that destroy us and afflict us? How can we apply Uzziah's experience in our own lives and always remember the Lord in all we do? These are the same questions I ask myself.

In light of Uzziah's story, let us consider one aspect of the covenant that we renew weekly when we partake of the sacrament—the promise to always remember the Savior (see Doctrine and Covenants 20:77, 79). This phrasing is repeated in both sacrament prayers. An important word in this covenant is *remember*.

The word *remember* is constantly used in the scriptures. It appears hundreds of times in them. In ancient Israel, the word *remember* was used in many instances to help the Lord's people to remember what He had done for them in times past.

It was even more commonly used in the context of covenants the Lord made with His people.

The children of Israel, like many today, had a difficult time remembering the Lord and His commandments, and because of their forgetting, they often suffered painful consequences. That is one of the reasons the Lord used the word *remember*. For example, the journey to Israel from Egypt began with a commandment to "remember this day, in which ye came out from Egypt, out of the house of bondage; for by strength of hand the Lord brought you out from this place" (Exodus 13:3).

The word *remember* comes from the Latin word *memor* and means "to be mindful of," and *re-* means "again." In this context, the word *remember* means to have in or to be able to bring to one's mind an awareness of someone or something that one has seen, known, or experienced in the past.[4] There is a strong correlation between the emotion felt and the resulting memory. Thus, the stronger the emotion, the more vivid and influential is the memory. In the Hebrew context, the word *remember* involves a knowledge that is accompanied by appropriate action. Thus, "doing" is an essential part of the remembering.

That is exactly what happened with Uzziah, the king of Judah, isn't it? Even Uzziah's own name reminded him where he was to turn for help during his life as he made decisions.

In summary, the more we remember the Lord, the more power we will have to keep on the path doing what the Lord expects from us, the more we will feel His love sustaining us, and the more we will naturally extend that love to everyone around us. In this sense, when we partake of the sacrament, we witness unto God, the Eternal Father, that we will remember the Savior in our mind and in our heart at all times and in all places. We promise that we will keep in our hearts vivid emotions and feelings of gratitude for His sacrifice, His love, and His gifts for us. We also promise that we will act upon these memories, feelings, and emotions.

One year after the beginning of the Restoration of The Church of Jesus Christ of Latter-day Saints, the Lord gave to Joseph Smith a revelation that is found in section 59 of the Doctrine and Covenants. This section gives a broader dimension to the covenant to always remember Him. This is what the Lord instructed Joseph Smith:

"Thou shalt offer a sacrifice unto the Lord thy God in righteousness, even that of a broken heart and a contrite spirit. And that thou mayest more fully keep thyself unspotted from the world, thou shalt go to the house of prayer and offer up thy sacraments upon my holy day; . . . Nevertheless thy vows shall be offered up in righteousness on all days and at all times; but remember that on this, the Lord's day, thou shalt offer thine oblations and thy sacraments unto the Most High, confessing thy sins unto thy brethren, and before the Lord" (Doctrine and Covenants 59:8–9, 11–12).

Through this revelation the Lord taught us about the why, the how, and the what to do to always remember Him. The why: to "fully keep thyself unspotted from the world." The how: that "thy vows shall be offered up in righteousness" with "a broken heart and a contrite spirit." And, finally, the what: to "offer thine oblations and thy sacraments unto the Most High, confessing thy sins unto thy brethren, and before the Lord."

This scripture mentions the word *oblations.* In the scriptures, the word *oblation* implies a full devotion to the Lord, offering Him a broken heart and a contrite spirit. It also means any sacrifice we make for the Lord. Thus the covenant of always remembering Him relates to sacrificing everything for the Lord with a broken heart and a contrite spirit. All this confirms that remembering the Savior is to act upon the things that will keep us on the path to righteousness.

What a priceless gift of compassion is given to us as we partake of the emblems of the broken body and the shed blood of the Master on His Sabbath day. As we partake of the sacrament, we eat the broken bread in remembrance of His body. We drink the water in remembrance of His blood that was shed for us. And we covenant with the Lord that we will always remember Him. We then receive the marvelous promise to "always have his Spirit to be with [us]" if we act upon our

covenant (Doctrine and Covenants 20:77). Partaking of the sacrament is regarded with such importance by our Heavenly Father that we are admonished to partake of it regularly every Sunday.

The covenant to always remember Him should influence and inspire us in every decision and action in our lives. King Benjamin in the Book of Mormon taught: "Therefore, I would that ye should take upon you the name of Christ, all you that have entered into the covenant with God that ye should be obedient unto the end of your lives. . . . And I would that ye should remember also, that this is the name that I said I should give unto you that never should be blotted out, except it be through transgression; therefore, take heed that ye do not transgress, that the name be not blotted out of your hearts" (Mosiah 5:8, 11).

Thus, remembering the Savior every single day affects every single decision we make, prompting us to always act with charity in our hearts. It affects, for example, how we speak; what we choose to do, to watch, to read, and to listen to; and how we treat one another. I can assure you that the Lord Himself will inspire these decisions, guide us in our challenges, fill our hearts with compassion, and assure that the harvest will be positive. As we remember the Savior daily, we won't be overcome by the influences and temptations that are conducting people away from the path of righteousness and leading them toward modern-day leprosies.

Given the reality of the Atonement of Jesus Christ, life has eternal and divine possibilities for those who always remember Him. It is of central importance to remember the feelings we have when we partake of the sacrament. We are preparing for eternal life and exaltation as we partake of the sacrament and promise to remember the Savior in our hearts and minds, knowing that remembering will help guide us in every decision and action.

I invite you to join me in reflecting on the impact this important principle can have in our personal lives. Please consider some of the things we can do to always remember Jesus Christ every single day. The Savior said, "Ye are my friends, if ye do whatsoever I command you" (John 15:14).

Our Savior Jesus Christ was motivated by His commitment to always remember the Father and to always do God's will because of His infinite love for God and for us. His sincere prayer in Gethsemane echoes in my mind: "Abba, Father, all things are possible unto thee; take away this cup from me: nevertheless not what I will, but what thou wilt" (Mark 14:36).

So many of the actions of our Savior in performing His infinite sacrifice and making covenants with us demonstrate His perfect love. Paraphrasing the words of the hymn "I Stand All Amazed," composed by Charles H. Gabriel, I declare to you that I stand all amazed by the moment when Jesus was nailed to the cross, and, while suffering extreme agony, He said, "Father, forgive them; for they know not what they do" (Luke 23:34).

I stand all amazed that for me He was crucified, that for me, a sinner, He suffered, He bled, He died, and He was resurrected. And He promised me that if I have a contrite spirit, acknowledging my sins and shortcomings, and if I am willing to repent, loving God's children like the Savior, the Lord will guarantee my forgiveness and my place at His side. It is wonderful that, even for a man like me, there is a chance if I always remember Him.

As one of His ordained Apostles on earth, I invite you to always remember and recognize the Savior in your lives. Come unto Him; allow His influence to guide your thoughts, your feelings, and your decisions. Look to Him in moments of distress, in moments of difficulty, in moments of depression, and in moments of challenge. As you do, you will feel of the Savior's love and His real concern for your well-being. Please remember that happiness and peace in this life and in the world to come depend upon remembering the Savior and your covenants with Him daily.

I witness that if we put our trust in the Savior, in His love, and in His atoning sacrifice, then when we seek for His help, even in the things that are confusing us, Jehovah will be our strength and will help us, as He did for Uzziah before his fall. I invite you to feel His love and to have faith that He will come to you. He is near, and He will, indeed, come to you. He will always be with us. Let us always remember the Savior. Let us always remember His love. And once we partake of His everlasting compassion, let us reach out and share it with others.

Chapter 7

LEARNING AND TEACHING THE GOSPEL

As recorded in the book of Acts, Philip the evangelist taught the gospel to a certain Ethiopian who was a eunuch in charge of all the treasures belonging to the queen of Ethiopia (see Acts 8:27). While returning from worshipping in Jerusalem, he read the book of Isaiah. Compelled by the Spirit, Philip came closer to him and said, "Understandest thou what thou readest? And [the eunuch] said, How can I, except some man should guide me? . . . Then Philip opened his mouth, and began at the same scripture, and preached unto him Jesus" (Acts 8:30–31, 35).

The question asked by this Ethiopian man is a reminder of the divine mandate we all have to seek to learn and to teach one another the gospel of Jesus Christ. In fact, in the context of learning and teaching the gospel, we are sometimes like the Ethiopian—we need the help of a faithful and inspired teacher; and we are sometimes like Philip—we need to teach and strengthen others in their conversion. Both of these acts are essential to developing and demonstrating true Christlike compassion. If we genuinely love God and love our fellow man, we will naturally want to invite all to come unto Him.

Our purpose as we seek to learn and to teach the gospel of Jesus Christ must be to increase faith in God and in His divine plan of happiness as well as in Jesus Christ and His atoning sacrifice. We must strive for lasting conversion. Such increased faith and conversion will help us make and keep covenants with God, thus strengthening our desire to follow Jesus and producing a genuine spiritual transformation in us—in other words, transforming us into a new creature, as taught by the Apostle Paul in his epistle to the Corinthians (see 2 Corinthians 5:17). This transformation will bring us a happier, more productive, and healthier life and help us to maintain an eternal perspective. Isn't this exactly what happened to the Ethiopian eunuch after he learned about the Savior and was converted to His gospel? The scripture says that "he went on his way rejoicing" (Acts 8:39).

The commandment to learn the gospel and teach it to one another as an act of Christlike love is not new; it has been repeated from the beginning of human history. One example of this occurred while Moses and his people were in the plains of Moab before entering the promised land. Through Moses, the Lord instructed the people to learn the statutes and covenants they had received and to teach them to their posterity, many of whom had not personally experienced the crossing of the Red Sea or the revelation given on Mount Sinai.

Moses admonished his people: "Hearken, O Israel, unto the statutes and unto the judgments, which I teach you, for to do them, that ye may live, and go in and possess the land which the Lord God of your fathers giveth you. . . . Teach them thy sons, and thy sons' sons" (Deuteronomy 4:1, 9).

Then Moses concluded, saying, "Thou shalt keep therefore his statutes, and his commandments, which I command thee this day, that it may go well with thee, and with thy children after thee, and that thou mayest prolong thy days upon the earth, which the Lord thy God giveth thee, for ever" (Deuteronomy 4:40).

God's prophets have consistently instructed that we need to raise our families "in the nurture and admonition of the Lord" (Ephesians 6:4) and "in light and truth" (Doctrine and Covenants 93:40). President Russell M. Nelson said, "In this day of rampant immorality and addictive pornography, parents have a sacred responsibility to teach their children the importance of God [and Jesus Christ] in their lives."[1]

The warning of our beloved prophet is a further reminder of our individual responsibility to seek to learn and also to teach our families that there is a Father in Heaven who loves us and who has developed a divine plan of happiness for His children; that Jesus Christ, His Son, is the Redeemer of the world; and that salvation comes from faith in His name. Our lives need to be rooted upon the rock of our Redeemer, Jesus Christ, which might help us individually and as families to have our own spiritual impressions engraved in our hearts, helping us to endure in our faith.

You may recall that two disciples of John the Baptist followed Jesus Christ after hearing John witness that Jesus was the Lamb of God, the Messiah. These good men accepted Jesus's invitation to "come and see" and abode with Him that day (see John 1:38–39). They came to know that Jesus was the Messiah, the Son of God, and followed Him for the rest of their lives.

Likewise, when we accept the Savior's invitation to "come and see," we need to abide in Him, immersing ourselves in the scriptures, rejoicing in them, learning His doctrine, and striving to live the way He lived. Only then will we come to know Jesus Christ and recognize His voice, knowing that as we come unto Him and believe in Him, we shall never hunger nor thirst. We will be able to discern truth and grow in our knowledge of the Lord, as occurred to those two disciples who abode with Jesus that day.

This doesn't happen by chance. Attuning ourselves to the highest influences of godliness is not a simple matter; it requires calling upon God and learning how to bring the gospel of Jesus Christ to the center of our lives. As we do so, I promise that the influence of the Holy Ghost will bring truth to our heart and mind and will bear witness of it, teaching all things (see John 14:26).

The Ethiopian's question, "How can I [understand], except some man should guide me?" also has a special meaning in the context of our individual responsibility to put the principles of the gospel we have learned into practice in our lives. In the Ethiopian's case, for example, he acted upon the truth he learned from Philip. He asked to be baptized. He came to know that Jesus Christ was the Son of God (see Acts 8:37–38).

Our actions must reflect what we learn and teach. We need to show our beliefs through the way we live. The best teacher is a good role model. Teaching something that we ourselves live can make a difference in the hearts of those we teach. If we desire for people, whether they are family or not, to joyfully treasure up the scriptures and the teachings of living apostles and prophets of our day, they need to see our souls delighting in them. Likewise, if we want them to know that the prophet is the seer and revelator in our day, they need to see us raise our hands to sustain him and see that we follow his inspired teachings. As the well-known American saying goes, "Actions speak louder than words."

Maybe you are at this exact moment thinking to yourself, "I have been doing all these things and have been following this model both individually and as a family, but unfortunately, some of my friends or dear ones have distanced themselves from the Lord. What should I do?" For those of you who are right now experiencing these feelings of sadness, agony, and sorrow, please know that your friends and dear ones are not totally lost because the Lord knows where they are and is watching over them. Remember, they are His children too!

It is hard to understand all the reasons why some people take another path. The best we can do in these circumstances is to love and embrace them, pray for their well-being, and seek for the Lord's help to know what to do and say. Sincerely rejoice with them in their successes; be their friends and look for the good in them. We should never give up on them. It is wise to preserve relationships by not rejecting or misjudging them. Just love them! The parable of the prodigal son teaches us that when children come to themselves, they often desire to come home. If that happens with your dear ones, fill your hearts with compassion, run to them, fall on their neck, and kiss them, like the father of the prodigal son did (see Luke 15:20).

Ultimately, all you can do is to keep living a worthy life, be a good example to others of what you believe, and draw closer to our Savior, Jesus Christ. He knows and understands your deep sorrows and pains, and He will bless your efforts and dedication to your dear ones if not in this life, in the next life. Remember that hope is an important part of the gospel plan.

Throughout many years of service in the Church, I have seen faithful members who have consistently applied these principles in their lives. This is the case of a single mother whom I will refer to as "Mary." Sadly, Mary went through a tragic divorce. At that point in time, Mary recognized that her most critical decisions relating to her family would be spiritual. She had to ask herself whether praying, scripture study, fasting, and church and temple attendance would continue to be important to her.

Mary had always been faithful, and at that critical juncture, she decided to cling to what she already knew to be true. She found strength in "The Family: A Proclamation to the World," which, among many wonderful principles, teaches that "parents have a sacred duty to rear their children in love and righteousness" and to teach them to always observe God's commandments. She continually searched for answers from the Lord and shared them with her four children in every family setting. They frequently discussed the gospel and shared their experiences and testimonies with one another.

Despite the sorrows they went through, her children developed a love for Christ's gospel and a desire to serve and share it with others. All four of them faithfully served full-time missions. Her oldest daughter, who is now married and strong in her faith, shared, "I never felt like my mom raised us alone because the Lord was always in our home. As she bore her witness of Him to us, we each began to turn to Him with our own questions. I am so grateful she brought the gospel to life."

This good mother was able to make her home a center of spiritual learning. Similar to the Ethiopian's question, Mary asked herself several times, "How can my children learn except a mother should guide them?"

When we earnestly, heartily, firmly, and sincerely seek to learn the gospel of Jesus Christ and teach it to one another with real purpose and under the influence of the Spirit, these teachings may transform hearts and inspire a desire to live according to the truths of God. We demonstrate our love for our Father in Heaven and for all of His children as we boldly proclaim the truth of His gospel and recognize the marvelous gift of the restored Church of Jesus Christ.

Chapter 8

SCRIPTURES AND PROPHETS: TESTAMENTS OF CHRIST'S LOVE

One of the signs of Christ's immense love for us is the fact that we are blessed with His words through the scriptures and through the teachings of living prophets in our day. Some believe that God once spoke to man but that the heavens are now silent. I submit that a compassionate Heavenly Father, a God who loves His children, would not pour out loving revelation on one group of His children and then sit in silent stoicism for the remainder of human history. Knowing our nature and our divine promises, a compassionate Father in Heaven would not leave us alone on this earth without direction, guidance, and communication with Him. He wants us to overcome our challenges, become better people, and return to live with Him and His Son Jesus Christ after this life. He wants us to find peace and joy in our journey as we prepare to receive these great promises.

As an act of compassion, God follows a pattern established from the beginning of guiding His children with multiple sources of direction both as a whole Church—through living prophets, seers, and revelators—and individually, through personal revelation often received after dedicated fasting, prayer, and study. He has provided us a Savior whose bowels are full of compassion and who has spoken to us from ancient times as recorded in the scriptures and through modern revelations given to His prophets. As I consider upon God's involvement with His people throughout the course of history, I reflect upon the book of Isaiah, which is an account of many difficulties and much wickedness among God's people. But Isaiah's powerful testimony of the love of the Savior echoes through his account: "Fear thou not; for I am with thee: be not dismayed; for I am thy God: I will strengthen thee; yea, I will help thee; yea, I will uphold thee with the right hand of my righteousness" (Isaiah 41:10). We have a Savior who can and does involve Himself in our lives in a personal, compassionate way. Although we live in a time when much difficulty and wickedness abound, I testify that His hand upholds each and every one of us, who He loves and cares for deeply.

While meeting with the elders of the Church on one occasion, the Prophet Joseph Smith declared: "Take away the Book of Mormon, and the revelations, and where is our religion? We have none."[1] Following the First Vision, the miraculous coming forth of the Book of Mormon is the second fundamental milestone of the unfolding Restoration of the gospel of Jesus

Christ in this dispensation. The Book of Mormon testifies of God's love for His children, of the Lord Jesus Christ's selfless and divine atoning sacrifice, and of His crowning ministry among the Nephites soon after His Resurrection. It provides essential direction for our lives and invites revelation from the Spirit. Indeed, revealed scripture becomes a loving message to each of us from our Savior.

As we study the coming forth of this holy book of scripture in these latter days, we come to realize that the entire undertaking was miraculous—from the Prophet Joseph receiving the gold plates from a holy angel to its translation "by the gift and power of God,"[2] its preservation by the hand of the Lord, and its publication. Its very existence is a powerful demonstration of the generous love of our Heavenly Father for His children.

The historical facts and the special witnesses of the Book of Mormon testify that its coming forth was indeed miraculous. Nevertheless, the power of this book is not based only in its magnificent history but on its powerful, unparalleled message that is a magnificent gift to the world and has changed countless lives—including mine!

I read the entire Book of Mormon for the first time when I was a young seminary student. As recommended by my teachers, I started reading it beginning with its introduction pages. The promise contained in the first pages of the Book of Mormon still echoes in my mind: "Ponder in [your] hearts . . . ,

and then . . . ask God . . . [in faith] . . . in the name of Christ if the book is true. Those who pursue this course and ask in faith will gain a testimony of its truth and divinity by the power of the Holy Ghost."[3]

With that loving promise in mind, earnestly seeking to know more about the truth of it, and in a spirit of prayer, I studied the Book of Mormon, little by little, as I completed the weekly assigned seminary lessons. I remember like it was yesterday that a warm feeling gradually began swelling in my soul and filling my heart, enlightening my understanding, and becoming more and more delightful, as described by Alma in his preaching the word of God to his people (see Alma 32:41-43). That feeling eventually turned into knowledge that took root in my heart and became the foundation of my testimony of the significant events and teachings found in this sacred book.

Through these and other priceless personal experiences, the Book of Mormon indeed became the keystone that sustains my faith in Jesus Christ and my testimony of the doctrine of His gospel. It became one of the pillars that testifies to me of Christ's divine atoning sacrifice and His infinite love for each of us. It became a shield throughout my life against the adversary's attempts to weaken my faith and instill disbelief in my mind and gives me courage to boldly declare my testimony of the Savior to the world.

My testimony of the Book of Mormon came line upon line as a miracle to my heart. To this day, this testimony continues to grow as I continuously search, with a sincere heart, to more fully understand the word of God as contained in this extraordinary book of scripture.

I invite you to be part of the marvelous coming forth of the Book of Mormon in your own life. I promise you that as you prayerfully and consistently study its words, you can partake of its promises and rich blessings in your life. I reaffirm once more the promise that echoes through its pages: that if you "ask God, the Eternal Father, in the name of Christ, if these things are not true; and if ye shall ask with a sincere heart, with real intent, having faith in Christ," He mercifully "will manifest the truth of it unto you, by the power of the Holy Ghost" (Moroni 10:4). I can assure you that our loving Father in Heaven will give you the answer in a very personal way, as He has done for me and many others around the world. Your experience will be as glorious and sacred for you as Joseph Smith's experiences were for him, as well as for all who have sought to receive a witness of the integrity and trustworthiness of this sacred book.

When I ponder what I read in the Book of Mormon and in other books of scripture, I often find myself reflecting on the feelings Nephi expressed after the death of his father: "For my soul delighteth in the scriptures, and my heart pondereth them, and writeth them for the learning and the profit of my children" (2 Nephi 4:15). Nephi went to the scriptures to be comforted after an incredibly difficult experience, and as promised, God did bless him with a profound outpouring of comfort and love. Like Nephi, delighting in the scriptures fills my heart with a deep awareness of my Savior's love and helps me to feel closer to Him. Feeling that love gives me encouragement, direction, comfort, and strength. Revealed truth in the scriptures answers the deep questions of my soul and makes me a new and a better man. I find myself intentionally striving to be better and to become what I am studying: a more loving, compassionate, and giving person. Simply put, I come to know my Savior better, because He is the personification of these attributes. Can you see in your own experiences that a life that is filled with light from revealed truth is much more fulfilling and motivating?

The Book of Mormon is indeed the word of God, and each page bears witness of His love for us. This sacred record "puts forth the doctrines of the gospel, outlines the plan of salvation, and tells men what they must do to gain peace in this life and eternal salvation in the life to come."[4] The Book of Mormon is God's instrument to bring about the gathering of Israel in our day and to help people come to know His Son, Jesus Christ, that each of us might feel Their everlasting love. Truly this miraculous book of scripture reveals the Lord's compassion for His children.

The Book of Mormon and other scriptures connect us with the teachings of prophets from long ago. Though their counsel is as timely now as it ever was, as "God is the same yesterday, today, and forever" (Mormon 9:9), isn't it a blessing to have prophets, seers, and revelators on earth in *these days* in which we live, who seek to know the will of the Lord and follow it? It is comforting to know that we are not alone in the world, despite the challenges we face in life. Having prophets is a sign of God's love for His children. They make known the promises and the true nature of God and of Jesus Christ to Their people. Having living prophets on the earth today is a sure sign of the Savior's love for us and His desire to bring to pass our eternal happiness.

Years ago, my wife and I received a phone call from President James E. Faust, then Second Counselor in the First Presidency. He called us to serve as mission president and companion in Portugal. He told us that we had only six weeks before we started the mission. Although we felt unprepared and inadequate, we accepted the call. Our most important concern at the time was to obtain the visas required to serve in that country because, according to past experience, we knew the process typically took six to eight months to complete.

President Faust then asked if we had faith that the Lord would perform a miracle and that we would be able to solve the visa problem faster. Our answer was a big yes, and we started making the arrangements immediately. We prepared the documents required for the visas, took our three young children, and went to the consulate as fast as we could. A very nice lady met with us there. In reviewing our papers and getting familiar with what we were going to do in Portugal, she turned to us and asked, "Are you really going to help the people of my country?" We firmly answered yes and explained that we would represent Jesus Christ, seeking to extend His love to all as we testified of Him and His divine mission in the world. We returned there four weeks later, received our visas, and landed in the mission field within the six weeks, as a prophet of the Lord had asked us to do.

From the bottom of my heart, I testify that the prophets speak by the power of the Holy Spirit. They testify of Christ and His divine mission on earth. They represent the mind and heart of the Lord and are called to represent Him and teach us what we must do to return to live in the presence of God and His Son, Jesus Christ. We are blessed as we exercise our faith and follow their teachings. By following them, our lives are happier and less complicated, our difficulties and problems are easier to bear, we are better able to love and serve as Christ would have us do, and we create a spiritual armor around us that will protect us from the attacks of the enemy in our day.

I once had a very interesting experience that illustrates this truth. I was on an assignment in a location where I had never been before. I got my GPS, input my destination address, and started following the directions. As I was approaching the destination, the GPS started giving me directions that seemed a little odd. I then decided to turn the GPS off because I thought I could find my destination myself. I soon realized that I was going in the wrong direction. Without the guidance of my GPS, I got lost and could not find my destination as I thought I could. I then stopped and turned the GPS on again and restarted following its directions. Fortunately, I repented in time and was able to reroute my direction. This time I followed each direction I received from my GPS. Eventually, I found my way, and I was able to worship with the members of the Church and enjoy the Spirit of the Lord in that special meeting and assignment I had been given.

This little experience reminded me of God's mercy and compassion for us, His children. He sent us here for this mortal experience with the purpose of getting us to our final destination, but He did not leave us without direction. Metaphorically speaking, God in His infinite love has provided various spiritual GPSes for us so we can walk through this mortal life and get to our final destination, which is to

live with Him and His son Jesus Christ. Unlike GPSes that we have here on earth that sometimes do fail us, the spiritual GPSes He provides us are unfailing and have a 100 percent guarantee of getting us safely to our destination.

One of the spiritual GPSes that God has made available for us is the teaching of Jesus Christ as revealed to His ancient and modern prophets. One of the glorious messages of the Restoration of The Church of Jesus Christ of Latter-day Saints is that God continues to speak to His children as He did in ancient times!

Like the prophets of old, prophets today testify of Jesus Christ and teach His gospel. A Christ-centered Church relies on a prophetic foundation to bless God's children in all times, but especially in times of adversity or danger—times when we might feel like children, confused or disoriented, and sometimes, perhaps a little fearful. What a gift of love it is from our Savior to ensure we have seers to guide us through even the darkest of times.

The First Presidency and Quorum of the Twelve are commissioned by God to be "special witnesses of the name of Christ" and have been given authority, through priesthood keys, to be those witnesses of Him (Doctrine and Covenants 107:23). You need to know that we love Him and we want the whole world to know the joy and love that come from following Him.

We can always trust the goodness and intentions of the living prophets. The Lord Himself declared: "What I the Lord have spoken, I have spoken, and I excuse not myself; and though the heavens and the earth pass away, my word shall not pass away, but shall all be fulfilled, whether by mine own voice or by the voice of my servants, it is the same" (Doctrine and Covenants 1:38). One passage in Second Chronicles that really impresses reads: "Believe in the Lord your God so shall ye be established; believe his prophets, so shall ye prosper" (2 Chronicles 20:20). Through declarations like these, the Lord is assuring us that God desires that all of His children listen to and heed His voice. His prophets are dedicated to helping us build our faith in Jesus Christ. Much of what the Lord reveals to His prophets amounts to an act of compassion intended to prevent sorrow for us as individuals and as societies.

Our greatest safety lies in following the words of the Lord as revealed to His prophets, especially in a world that is getting more confusing. Mortal life is full of distractions and detours, especially in these latter days. We are surrounded by all kinds of modern-day social pressures, loud voices, and social media opinions that encourage us to turn off our spiritual GPS and look for guidance elsewhere or blaze our own trail. We put ourselves in spiritual danger when we trust only our own wisdom and turn off this spiritual GPS. Therefore, following the words of the Lord and His prophets is not only an issue of

convenience, but more importantly, it is a means of spiritual survival. In addressing the whole Church, President Nelson declared: "The Lord always has and always will instruct and inspire His prophets. The Lord is at the helm!" What a blessing. "We who have been ordained to bear witness of His holy name throughout the world will continue to seek to know His will and follow it."[5]

Striving to follow the counsel of living prophets has truly made a difference in my life as I have sought to know the Lord's will for me. It has helped me to establish my way of being not only as a member and leader in the restored Church of Jesus Christ, but also as a father, a husband, and a participant in my professional career. It has also helped me to look for ways to constantly improve myself. The gift of having a living prophet has blessed my life at every major milestone and in every quiet moment of reflection.

Since the beginning of our marriage, my wife and I have committed together to follow the teachings of our prophets, no matter what circumstances we face. That decision has brought us closer to the Lord and blessed us immensely. As you approach major decisions in your life, I would encourage you to make that same commitment. Study the words of the prophets to help you in your decisions! Modern technology makes their words very accessible and also searchable. I promise that as you make an effort to seek out and follow prophetic counsel, you will be led in your search to specific direction that will be pertinent and helpful to you in your individual situation.

A friend of mine once called me and shared with me that he was questioning the teachings of our current prophets. He told me that he was in the middle of a faith crisis, as he put it, and he wondered how he could really believe in the words of prophets. I responded to his comments with a question for his consideration: "How could I deny the feelings, blessings, and testimony that I have felt throughout my life as I follow the words of prophets of our day?" Concerning the questions he had, I told him that I chose to cling to what I already knew and not to what I don't. You might be struggling with your own faith in God and in His Son, Jesus Christ, or even in the teachings and counsel of His prophets. I know people who have chosen to follow another path. This does not make them bad people. However, I want to help you see that those paths, while tempting, can lead us to undue stress, heartache, and grief, similar to what I experienced when I turned off my GPS trying to find my way on my own that day. God loves you, I assure you, and He does everything He can to keep you close to Him. One of the ways He expresses His love for us is by continuing to reveal His will to us through living prophets. And one of the ways we express our love for Him is by following His chosen prophets.

As I reflect on how blessed we are to have living prophets on earth in our day, another personal experience comes to mind. Before my call as an Apostle, I accompanied Elder D. Todd Christofferson to Yaoundé, a beautiful city located in the country of Cameroon, in central Africa. Due to multiple flight delays, we landed in Yaoundé later than planned, and we were set to depart for South Africa in the early evening.

A devotional was planned for noon that day, and members were invited to come if their schedules would allow. Due to the unusual meeting time, we expected there to be a very small number of Saints in attendance, but Elder Christofferson felt a strong desire to take that opportunity to be among any who were able to come. To our surprise, when we arrived, the auditorium was filled to capacity. Following the meeting, Elder Christofferson greeted each person individually. Watching these faithful members greet a prophet of God is something I will never forget. Some would grasp his extended hand for quite some time; others would kiss his palm and hold his hand to their face. Some would simply reach out and touch his clothing in love and awe, reminding me of the woman who touched the clothing of the Savior in order to find strength and healing. Each greeting was warm and filled with the Spirit. Truly, these good members were experiencing the loving compassion of the Lord through His servants, and their hearts were filled with love for one another in turn.

One man in particular, who came with his two children, mentioned that his children were supposed to have been in school that day, but he emphatically said, "How could I send them to school when they had the opportunity to come here and be with a prophet of God?" I hope this good man's testimony will live on in the hearts of his children, as it has lived on in my heart. Do we fully realize the blessing it is to have living prophets on the earth today?

Much of what has happened and is happening in my life and our life as a family is a result of the application of what we have learned from our prophets, seers, and revelators as they reveal the Lord's love and concern for us. I assure you that "for those diligently seeking eternal life, the prophet's voice brings spiritual safety in very turbulent times."[6] Following the teachings of our prophets is one of the most important "spiritual GPSes" available to help us find our final destination in the presence of God and Jesus Christ, and calling prophets to represent His voice on earth today is one of our Savior's most compassionate gifts.

As an Apostle of the Lord Jesus Christ, I have a purpose to lovingly invite and help all to come unto Christ. I and the other members of the Quorum of the Twelve work tirelessly to find ways to strengthen the faith of people we meet as we are sent by the Savior Jesus Christ to minister to all.

I want to testify that the Lord speaks to each of us through the holy scriptures and through His modern prophets and apostles, and that He does so because of His great compassion for each of us. Everything I have found in my personal study of the scriptures and in the teachings of modern-day prophets is evidence and reassurance of the Lord's pure compassion for me, personally, and for all His children. The scriptures are a witness of His desire to communicate, guide, lead, and encourage His children to be of one mind and heart. There is a reason that in the first book of Nephi the iron rod is representative of the Word of God, because God's words, whether through ancient scripture or through modern-day prophets, lead us surely and directly down the covenant path. God's words invite us to partake of everlasting life and to receive the rich eternal blessings He has in store for each one of us.

I testify that in perfect love and as the head of His Church, Jesus has orchestrated the coming forth of the Book of Mormon and other sacred scripture and has called faithful and dedicated men to serve as prophets of God on earth today. They are a gift from a compassionate Savior to guide us back to Him. Let us follow their teachings, that we may find safety and peace and feel the loving embrace of our Savior Jesus Christ.

Chapter 9

THE GIFT OF REPENTANCE

Perhaps the perfect compassion and infinite love of the Savior were fully demonstrated in His Atonement. Through this singular event in human history, each of us received the unmatched gift of repentance—the opportunity to turn our hearts and lives to Him again and again as we inevitably falter in this mortal realm. Though this world is full of temptation and distraction, if we hold to the iron rod and rely upon our Savior's loving act of mercy, we will be strengthened and cleansed so that we might return to Him.

I am certain you have already heard of Michelangelo, the Italian sculptor. Besides being a sculptor, he was a painter, a poet, and an architect, and he is considered one of the foremost artists of Western civilization during the period of the Renaissance. He was born in Italy in 1475, and he is known as a genius for his large marble statues. He lived in Italy most of his life and left an artistic legacy for humanity that is admired even today.

One of his most famous sculptures is called the *Pietà*. This statue portrays the scene of Mary, the mother of Jesus, seated with Jesus Christ, her son, lying in her arms after having been taken down from the cross. Mary's countenance expresses profound sadness for the suffering that she has experienced, and the face of Jesus expresses the suffering He had been through after having borne the arduous burden of taking upon Him the sins of the world and being nailed to the cross. It is a work of art that depicts the authenticity of the physical and emotional details of a scene of suffering.

I had the privilege of viewing this sculpture during a visit I made to Saint Peter's Basilica in the Vatican. I was even more impressed to learn that Michelangelo used basically two main tools to accomplish his works of art: a hammer and a chisel. It is truly incredible to imagine how someone could create such an enormous and beautiful work of art from a piece of raw marble using these two tools. Certainly he was very talented and knew how to use the resources he had to produce such beautiful works of art.

When I think about the works he produced and the results he achieved, I think figuratively about the wonderful plan of love our Heavenly Father developed in consideration for each of us and for what He hoped we might become when He sent us here to earth.

Each of us was born with the potential to become like our Heavenly Father. Through our experiences and by properly using our agency and the gift of repentance, thus relying on "the merits, and mercy, and grace of the Holy Messiah," we can turn our lives in the direction of God and become like Him (see 2 Nephi 2:8). Or we can be distracted by the world and fail to achieve our potential as it was promised to us. Figuratively, we all have the potential to become beautiful works of art in the Lord's hands. In this sense, He is the sculptor and He molds us through our experiences day by day. If we allow the Lord to shape us by continually turning again to Him through repentance, the result will be wonderful.

Let us imagine that for some reason we have been deceived or confused by temptation and we end up sinning. Surely it will happen to each of us at some point. What should we do? If we fall into temptation and sin, we have to reconcile ourselves with God. In the language of the scriptures, this means we must repent.

Repentance is "a change of mind and heart that brings a fresh attitude toward God, oneself, and life in general. Repentance implies that a person turns away from evil and turns his heart and will to God, submitting to God's commandments and desires and forsaking sin. True repentance comes from a love for God and a sincere desire to obey his commandments."[1]

I like very much what Elder Neil L. Andersen has taught about repentance:

> When we sin, we turn away from God. When we repent, we turn back toward God.
>
> The invitation to repent is rarely a voice of chastisement but rather a loving appeal to turn around and to "re-turn" toward God [see Helaman 7:17]. It is the beckoning of a loving Father and His Only Begotten Son to be more than we are, to reach up to a higher way of life, to change, and to feel the happiness of keeping the commandments. Being disciples of Christ, we rejoice in the blessing of repenting and the joy of being forgiven. They become part of us, shaping the way we think and feel.[2]

Without a doubt, repentance is a wonderful gift that is available to all who desire to return to God. It is available to those who have the desire to hold on to the iron rod and allow the Lord to mold their lives into wonderful works of art. Repentance allows the Lord in His mercy to shape our lives and make us into beautiful works of art.

This process takes time. Michelangelo was thirteen years old when he began his artistic activities as an apprentice in Italy. He followed his masters' teachings, and for the majority

of his life he produced works of art admired around the world. Like Michelangelo, we need to understand that it is possible to shape our lives from one day to another.

Our choices shape our souls. Recognizing our dedication and perseverance, the Lord will show compassion on us and give us what we are unable to obtain by ourselves. He will shape us as He sees our efforts to overcome our imperfections and human weakness.

In that regard, repentance becomes part of our daily lives. Our weekly taking of the sacrament is so important—to come meekly, humbly before the Lord, acknowledging our dependence upon Him, asking Him to forgive and to renew us, and promising to always remember Him.

As we strive to make daily repentance a part of our lives, we replace the emptiness that comes from sin with the love that comes from the atoning sacrifice of our Savior Jesus Christ. His love has the capacity to fill our heart with joy beyond description, and experiencing this joy for ourselves enables us to appreciate more profoundly our Heavenly Father's infinite compassion and mercy for us. When Heavenly Father sent us to earth, He knew the path of mortality would not be easy and, in His wisdom, He compassionately offered us all the help we would need during our journey. Therefore He sent His Son to show us the way and to sacrifice His life for us so we could be redeemed from our sins and death. Part of our Savior's infinite sacrifice, as we read in Alma 7:12, was to take upon Himself our "infirmities, that his bowels may be filled with mercy, according to the flesh, that he may know according to the flesh how to succor (us) according to (our) infirmities."

As we experience this merciful, perfect compassion firsthand, we grow in love and gratitude for Jesus Christ and His Father, standing in awe of the grace They offer us. Naturally, as we appreciate Their infinite mercy more and more, we become patient and empathetic in our interactions with others, viewing each other's challenges and shortcomings with love and understanding rather than criticism. As we experience the Savior's atoning power for ourselves, we can become more Christlike.

Sometimes in our daily efforts to become more Christlike, we find ourselves repeatedly struggling with the same difficulties. It is as if we are climbing a tree-covered mountain. At times we don't see our progress until we get closer to the top and look back from the high ridges. Please don't be discouraged. If you are striving and working to repent, then you are in the process of repenting.

Elder D. Todd Christofferson stated, "Overcoming bad habits or addictions often means an effort today followed by another tomorrow and then another, perhaps for many days, even months and years, until we achieve victory."[3]

As we improve, we see life more clearly and feel the Holy Ghost working more strongly within us. For those who are truly repentant but seem unable to feel relief, continue keeping the commandments. I promise you, relief will come in the timetable of the Lord. Healing also requires time.

My invitation is for all of us to allow the Lord to mold and transform our lives into our potential—into that which our Heavenly Father has planned for us.

Let us understand our eternal perspective and turn our lives into beautiful works of art that were planned by a loving Heavenly Father who developed a plan of redemption so that we could return to His presence. Our returning is only possible through Jesus Christ, and His atoning sacrifice—the most majestic, most immeasurable, and most compassionate act that has occurred in all of human history.

The eminent words of the prophet Isaiah magnify the greatness and selflessness of the Savior's condescension and sacrifice in behalf of all the children of God: "Surely he hath borne our griefs, and carried our sorrows: yet we did esteem him stricken, smitten of God, and afflicted. But he was wounded for our transgressions, he was bruised for our iniquities: the chastisement of our peace was upon him; and with his stripes we are healed" (Isaiah 53:4–5).

By voluntarily taking upon Himself the sins of all mankind, being cruelly nailed to the cross, and victoriously conquering death on the third day, Jesus gave a more sacred significance to the Passover ordinance that had been bestowed upon Israel in ancient times. In fulfillment of prophecy, He offered His own body and precious blood as the great and last sacrifice, validating the traditional symbols used in the celebration of the Lord's Passover. In so doing, Christ experienced physical and spiritual suffering that is incomprehensible to the human mind.

The Savior Himself said: "For behold, I, God, have suffered these things for all . . . ; which suffering caused myself, even God, the greatest of all, to tremble because of pain, and to bleed at every pore, and to suffer both body and spirit—and would that I might not drink the bitter cup, and shrink—Nevertheless, glory be to the Father, and I partook and finished my preparations unto the children of men" (Doctrine and Covenants 19:16, 18–19).

Christ graciously and compassionately fulfilled the will of the Father through His infinite and merciful sacrifice. He overcame the sting of physical and spiritual death, introduced to the world through the Fall, offering us the glorious possibility of eternal salvation.

Jesus was the only Being capable of realizing this eternal and perfect sacrifice for all of us. He was chosen and foreordained in the Grand Council in Heaven, even before the world was formed (see 1 Peter 1:20; Moses 4:2). Furthermore, being born of a mortal mother, He inherited physical death, but as the Only Begotten Son of the Father, He inherited the power to lay down His own life and then take it up again (see John 10:18). Additionally, Christ lived a perfect life that was without blemish and, therefore, was exempt from the demands of divine justice (see Hebrews 4:15; 1 Peter 2:21–22).

The Prophet Joseph Smith taught: "Salvation could not come to the world without the mediation of Jesus Christ. God . . . prepared a sacrifice in the gift of His own Son, who should be sent in due time to . . . open a door through which man might enter into the Lord's presence."[4]

While through His sacrifice the Savior unconditionally removed the effects of physical death, He did not eliminate our personal responsibility to repent for the sins we commit. Rather, He extended to us a loving invitation to be reconciled to our Eternal Father. Through Jesus Christ and His atoning sacrifice, we can experience a mighty change of mind and heart, bringing a fresh attitude, both toward God and toward life in general. When we sincerely repent of our sins and turn our hearts and will to God and His commandments, we can receive His forgiveness and feel the influence of His Holy Spirit in greater abundance. Mercifully, we avoid having to experience the depth of suffering the Savior endured (see Doctrine and Covenants 19:15–18).

The gift of repentance is an expression of God's compassion toward His children, and it is a demonstration of His incomparable power to help us overcome the sins we commit. It is also an evidence of the patience and long-suffering our loving Father has for our mortal weakness and frailties. President Russell M. Nelson referred to this gift as "the key to happiness and peace of mind."[5]

As we genuinely repent of our sins, we allow the atoning sacrifice of Christ to become wholly effective in our life and demonstrate our love and gratitude for Him. We will become free from the bondage of sin, find joy in our earthly journey, and become eligible to receive eternal salvation, which was prepared from the foundation of the world for all who believe in Jesus Christ and come unto Him.

In addition to providing the majestic gift of salvation, the Savior offers us relief and comfort as we face our afflictions, temptations, and weaknesses of mortal life, including the circumstances we have experienced recently in the pandemic. I can assure you that Christ is ever aware of the adversities we experience in mortality. He understands all of the bitterness, agony, and physical pain as well as the emotional and spiritual challenges we face. The Savior's bowels are filled with mercy, and He is always ready to succor us. This is possible because He personally took upon Himself, in the flesh, the pain of our weaknesses and infirmities (see Alma 7:11–13).

With meekness and humility of heart, He descended below all things and accepted being despised, rejected, and humiliated by men, having been wounded for our transgressions and iniquities. He suffered these things for all, taking upon Himself the sins of the world, thus becoming our ultimate spiritual caregiver.

As we draw nearer to Him, surrendering ourselves spiritually to His care, we will be able to take upon ourselves His yoke, which is easy, and His burden, which is light, thus finding that promised comfort and rest (see Matthew 11:28–30). Furthermore, we will receive the strength we all need to overcome the hardships, weaknesses, and sorrows of life, which are exceedingly difficult to endure without His help and healing power. The scriptures teach us to "cast thy burden upon the Lord, and he shall sustain thee" (Psalm 55:22). "And then may God grant unto [us] that [our] burdens may be light, through the joy of his Son" (Alma 33:23).

Chapter 10

TAKING UP OUR CROSS AND FOLLOWING HIM

While in the vicinity of Caesarea Philippi, the Savior revealed to His disciples what He would suffer at the hands of the elders, chief priests, and scribes in Jerusalem. He specifically taught them about His death and glorious Resurrection (see Matthew 16:21). At that point in time, His disciples did not completely understand His divine mission on earth. Peter himself, when he heard what the Savior had said, took Him aside and rebuked Him, saying, "Be it far from thee, Lord: this shall not be unto thee" (v. 22).

To help His disciples understand that devotion to His work includes submission and suffering as an act of compassion, the Savior emphatically declared: "If any man will come after me, let him deny himself, and take up his cross, and follow me. For whosoever will save his life shall lose it: and whosoever will lose his life for my sake shall find it. For what is a man profited, if he shall gain the whole world, and lose his own soul? or what shall a man give in exchange for his soul?" (Matthew 16:24–26).

Through this declaration, the Savior emphasized that all those who are willing to follow Him need to deny themselves and control their desires, appetites, and passions, sacrificing everything, even life itself if necessary, being entirely submissive to the will of the Father—just as He did. This is, in fact, the price to be paid for the salvation of a soul. Jesus purposely and metaphorically used the symbol of a cross to help His disciples better understand what sacrifice and devotion to the Lord's cause would truly mean. The image of a cross was well known among His disciples and the inhabitants of the Roman Empire because Romans forced victims of crucifixion to publicly carry their own cross or crossbeam to the place where their execution would occur.

It was only after the Savior's Resurrection that the disciples' minds were opened to understand all that had been written about Him and what would be required of them from that time on.

In the same fashion, all of us need to open our minds and our hearts in order to more fully understand the relevance of taking upon ourselves our crosses and following Him. We learn through the scriptures that those who wish to take their cross upon themselves will love Jesus Christ in such a way that they deny themselves of all ungodliness and of every worldly lust and keep His commandments. As they do so, they also better fulfill the second great commandment, to love and serve others as Christ does.

Our determination to cast off all that is contrary to God's will, to sacrifice all we are asked to give, and to strive to follow His teachings will help us to endure in the path of Jesus Christ's gospel—even in the face of tribulation, the weakness of our souls, or the social pressure and worldly philosophies that oppose His teachings. Taking up our cross and steadfastly following Him allows us to both feel and express the abiding love of our Savior more deeply than we would otherwise.

For example, for those who do not currently have an eternal companion and may be feeling lonely or disappointed, I encourage you to accept the Savior's invitation to take upon yourselves your cross and follow Him as you continue with faith on the Lord's path, not indulging in worldly habits. This will help you maintain your hope in God's love and mercy.

These same principles apply to those who are experiencing same-gender attraction and might feel unsure of God's love and His plan for them. They may even feel that the gospel of Jesus Christ is not for them anymore. If that is the case for you, I want to assure you that there is always hope in God the Father and in His plan of happiness, in Jesus Christ and His atoning sacrifice, and in living Their loving commandments. In His perfect love, mercy, justice, and wisdom, the Lord may

seal us His, that we may be brought to His presence and have everlasting salvation, if we are steadfast and immovable in keeping the commandments (see Alma 1:25) and are always abounding in good works (see Mosiah 5:15).

To those who have committed serious sins, accepting this same invitation means, among other things, to humble yourself before God, to counsel with appropriate Church leaders, and to repent and forsake your sins. Remember that repentance is a gift of compassion and mercy given to us by a loving Father in Heaven. This process will also bless all who are fighting against debilitating addictions, including opioids and other drugs, alcohol, and pornography. Taking these steps brings you closer to the Savior, who can ultimately free you from guilt, sorrow, and spiritual and physical slavery. Additionally, you may desire to seek the support of your family, friends, and competent medical and counseling professionals.

Please never give up after subsequent failures or consider yourself incapable of abandoning sins and overcoming addiction. You cannot afford to stop trying and thereafter continue in weakness and sin! Always strive to do your best, manifesting through your works the desire to cleanse the inner vessel, as taught by the Savior. Sometimes solutions to certain challenges come after months and months of continuous effort. The promise found in the Book of Mormon that "it is by grace that we are saved, after all we can do" (2 Nephi 25:23) is applicable in these circumstances. Please remember that the Savior's gift of grace "is not necessarily limited in time to 'after' all we can do. We may receive His grace before, during, and after the time when we expend our own efforts."[1]

As we continually strive to overcome our challenges, God will bless us with the gifts of faith to be healed and of the working of miracles. He will compassionately do for us what we are not capable of doing for ourselves.

Additionally, for those who feel bitter, angry, offended, or chained to sorrows for something you feel is undeserved, to take up one's cross and follow the Savior means to strive to lay aside these feelings and turn to the Lord so He can free us from this state of mind and help us to find peace. Unfortunately, if we hold on to these negative feelings and emotions, we may find ourselves living without the influence of the Lord's Spirit in our lives. Remember, we cannot repent *for* other people, but we can forgive them—by refusing to be held hostage by those who have harmed us.[2]

The scriptures teach that there is a way out of these situations—by inviting our Savior to help us to replace our stony hearts with new hearts (see Ezekiel 18:31; 36:26). For this to happen, we need to come before the Lord with our weakness and implore His help and forgiveness, especially during the sacred moment when we partake of the sacrament each Sunday. May we choose to seek His help and take an

important and difficult step by forgiving those who have hurt us so that our wounds may begin to heal. I promise you that in your doing so, your nights will be full of the relief that comes from a mind at peace with the Lord.

While in Liberty Jail in 1839, the Prophet Joseph Smith wrote an epistle to Church members containing prophecies that are so very applicable in all these circumstances and situations. He wrote, "All thrones and dominions, principalities and powers, shall be revealed and set forth upon all who have endured valiantly for the gospel of Jesus Christ" (Doctrine and Covenants 121:29). Therefore, those who have taken upon themselves the name of the Savior, trusting in His promises and persevering to the end, will be saved and may dwell with God in a state of never-ending happiness (see Mosiah 2:41).

We all face adverse circumstances in our lives that make us feel sad, helpless, hopeless, and sometimes even weakened. Some of these feelings may lead us to question the Lord: "Why am I experiencing these situations?" or "Why are my expectations not met? After all, I am doing everything in my power to carry my cross and follow the Savior!"

We must remember that taking our cross upon ourselves includes being humble and trusting in God and in His infinite wisdom. We must acknowledge that He loves us and is aware of each of us and of our needs. It is also necessary to accept the fact that the Lord's timing is different than ours. Sometimes we seek for a blessing and set a time limit for the Lord to fulfill it. We cannot condition our faithfulness to Him by imposing a deadline for the answers to our desires. When we do this, we resemble the skeptical Nephites from ancient times, who mocked their brothers and sisters by saying that the time was past for the fulfillment of the words spoken by Samuel the Lamanite, creating confusion among those who believed (see 3 Nephi 1:4–7). We need to trust the Lord enough to be still and know that He is God, that He knows all things, and that He is aware of each of us.

I once had the opportunity to minister to a widowed sister named Franca Calamassi, who was suffering from a debilitating illness. Sister Calamassi was the first member of her family to join the restored Church of Jesus Christ. Although her husband was never baptized, he consented to meet with the missionaries and often attended Church meetings. Despite these circumstances, Sister Calamassi remained faithful and raised her four children in the gospel of Jesus Christ. A year following her husband's passing, Sister Calamassi took her children to the temple, and they participated in sacred ordinances and were sealed together as a family. The promises associated with these ordinances brought her much hope, joy, and happiness that helped her carry on in life.

When the first symptoms of Sister Calamassi's disease began to appear, her bishop gave her a blessing. At that time she

told her bishop that she was ready to accept the Lord's will, expressing her faith to be healed as well as her faith to endure her illness to the end.

During my visit, while holding Sister Calamassi's hand and looking into her eyes, I saw an angelic glow emanating from her countenance—reflecting her confidence in God's plan and her perfect brightness of hope in the Father's love and plan for her. I felt her firm determination to endure in her faith until the end by taking up her cross, despite the challenges she was facing. This sister's life is a testimony of Christ, a statement of her faith and devotion to Him.

Taking upon us our cross and following the Savior requires us to follow His example and strive to become like Him, patiently facing the circumstances of life, denying and despising the appetites of the natural man, waiting on the Lord, and feeling the Lord's compassion for us and sharing it with others. The Psalmist wrote: "Wait on the Lord: be of good courage, and he shall strengthen thine heart: wait, I say, on the Lord" (Psalm 27:14). "He is our help and our shield" (Psalm 33:20).

I testify to you that following our Master's footsteps and waiting on Him who is the ultimate healer of our lives will provide rest to our souls and make our burdens easy and light (see Matthew 11:30).

Chapter 11

PATHS FOR HAPPINESS

We learn through the scriptures of our Heavenly Father's purpose for His children: "This is my work and my glory—to bring to pass the immortality and eternal life of man" (Moses 1:39). A Gospel Topics essay states, "Heavenly Father desires that we find true, lasting happiness. Our happiness is the design of all the blessings He gives us—gospel teachings, commandments, priesthood ordinances, family relationships, prophets, temples, the beauties of creation, and even the opportunity to experience adversity. His plan for our salvation is often called 'the great plan of happiness' [Alma 42:8]. He sent His Beloved Son to carry out the Atonement so we can be happy in this life and receive a fulness of joy in the eternities."[1] Surely, everything about who God is and what He sent Christ to do demonstrates Their supreme love and compassion for each of us. And if we are to accept and receive of God's love, we should consider doing what we can to fulfill His work and His glory—including seeking after true happiness.

As you take your next steps in life's great adventure, I invite you to consider ways to find the paths of true happiness in life. When we look around the world, it is very obvious that people everywhere are looking for something. In their own way, what they are really looking for is happiness. However, like the gospel itself, these people "are only kept from [happiness] because they know not where to find it" (Doctrine and Covenants 123:12). Because they do not know where to find true and lasting happiness, they try to find it in ways that will actually only bring temporary pleasure—such as buying things, seeking honor and praise from the world through inappropriate behavior, and focusing on physical beauty and attractiveness. Pleasure is often confused with happiness, but it is by no means synonymous with it. It seems that the more people seek this kind of temporary pleasure, the less and less happy they actually become. Pleasure, unlike happiness, is that which pleases us or gives us gratification. Usually, it endures for only a short time. As President David O. McKay once said, "You may get that transitory pleasure, yes, but you cannot find joy, you cannot find happiness. Happiness is found only along that well-beaten track, narrow as it is, though straight, which leads to life eternal."[2]

Studies show that people are experiencing less happiness in life in the United States of America.³ Unfortunately for many, happiness is an elusive state. Scientists know happiness is "more than simply positive mood, happiness is a state of well-being that encompasses living a good life, one with a sense of meaning and deep satisfaction."⁴

Recent research has shown that happiness is not the result of bouncing from one experience to the next. Instead, achieving happiness typically involves a long-sustained effort for something more important in life. Happiness is determined by habits, behaviors, and thought patterns that we can directly address with intentional action. Studies suggest that these most important determining factors in achieving true happiness are actually "under personal control."⁵

It would be worthwhile and beneficial to consider the importance of some of the paths for happiness as taught in the scriptures and by modern prophets and apostles. My intent is to bring these paths into our minds and hearts so we can make sure our footsteps are faithfully and firmly rooted in them. Doing so will allow us to truly enjoy happiness in the journey that is ahead.

The first of these paths is the path of virtue. Why is virtue so important in the path of happiness? Virtue is a pattern of thought and behavior based on high moral standards; it encompasses chastity and moral purity that prequalifies you to enter the Lord's holy temples. Virtuous people possess a quiet dignity and inner strength. They are confident because they are worthy to receive and be guided by the Holy Ghost. Virtue begins in the heart and in the mind, and it is the accumulation of thousands of small decisions and actions each day.

In Doctrine and Covenants 121:45–46 we read: "Let virtue garnish thy thoughts unceasingly; then shall thy confidence wax strong in the presence of God; and the doctrine of the priesthood shall distil upon thy soul as the dews from heaven. The Holy Ghost shall be thy constant companion, and thy scepter an unchanging scepter of righteousness and truth; and thy dominion shall be an everlasting dominion, and without compulsory means it shall flow unto thee forever and ever."

President Russell M. Nelson has taught: "Eternal principles that govern happiness apply equally to all. I doubt that the Lord cares much which honorable vocation you pursue. But He does care if you love one another and serve one another (see Mosiah 4:15). And He cares that you have the obedience and self-discipline needed to maintain your identity and honor your highest priorities."[6]

A second path for happiness is uprightness. Elder Richard G. Scott once taught: "Recognize that enduring happiness comes from what you are, not from what you have. Real joy comes from righteous character, and that is built from a pattern of consistent righteous decisions. When the things that you

acquire are used as tools to help others, they won't rule your life. Your righteous decisions determine who you are and what is important to you. They make doing the right things easier. For happiness now and throughout your life, steadfastly obey the Lord, no matter what pressure you feel to do otherwise."[7] As we study the scriptures, we learn that the promises made by the Lord to us encourage righteous living. Those promises must nourish our soul, bringing us hope by encouraging us not to give up even in the face of our daily challenges of living in a world where ethical and moral values are becoming extinct, thus motivating people to sow in the flesh. Therefore, we need to make sure that our thoughts, words, and actions are elevating us to the level of the divinity of our heavenly parents.

A third path for happiness is faithfulness. It is fundamental to understand that God blesses us according to our faith. Faith is the source of living with divine purpose and eternal perspective. Faith is a practical principle that inspires diligence. It is a vital, living force manifested in our positive attitude and our desire to willingly do everything that God and Jesus Christ ask of us. It's what takes us to our knees to implore the Lord for guidance and encourages us to arise and act with confidence to achieve things consistent with His will. Dear friends, as you go forward in your journey of faith, you will likely go through periods of testing where you will be tried to see if you will do all things that the Lord your God shall command you. This is part of the mortal life experience. This will require unwavering faith in Christ—even in times of great difficulty. It will require that you press forward with steadfast faith in Christ, being led by the Spirit and trusting that God will provide for your needs. Please remember that you will need to be steadfast and that you must not waver in your faith. As you do so, the Lord will increase your capacity to rise above the challenges of life.

A fourth path for happiness is holiness. Holiness is related to spiritual and moral perfection. Holiness indicates purity of a person's heart and intent. The question is, what can we do each day to feed ourselves spiritually to the point that we can develop such godly character? President Harold B. Lee, one of the prophets of this dispensation, answered this question. He said: "We develop our spiritual selves by practice. . . . We must have daily exercise by our spirits by prayer, by doing daily good deeds, by sharing with others. We must feed our spirits daily by studying the scriptures every day, by [family home evening], by attendance at meetings, by the partaking of the sacrament. . . . The righteous man strives for self-improvement knowing that he has daily need of repentance for his misdeeds or his neglect. . . . He endeavors to make each day his masterpiece so that at night's close he can witness in his soul and to his God that whatever has come to his hand that day, he has done to the best of his ability."[8]

Another important element of holiness is related to making and keeping covenants in the temple. If we are faithful to these covenants, they can take us beyond the limits of our own power and perspective. All the promised blessings of the gospel of Jesus Christ will be ours through our faithfulness to the ordinances and covenants we make before God and Jesus Christ in the temple. The people of Nephi "lived after the manner of happiness." Part of their pattern of living included building a temple in which to worship and make covenants with the Lord (see 2 Nephi 5:16, 27).

A key element of the path of holiness is that we should be sure to develop spirituality and be morally pure. We read in Doctrine and Covenants 20:69: "And the members shall manifest before the church, and also before the elders, by a godly walk and conversation, that they are worthy of it, that there may be works and faith agreeable to the holy scriptures—walking in holiness before the Lord."

Finally, a fifth path for happiness involves keeping all the commandments of God, which is related to all the other paths I have mentioned. After the Nephites were separated from the Lamanites, they prospered exceedingly, for they did observe to keep the judgments, and the statutes, and the commandments of the Lord in all things, according to the law of Moses (see 2 Nephi 5:10–11). This pattern was an important element of living after the manner of happiness (v. 27).

President Thomas S. Monson once taught: "When we keep the commandments, our lives will be happier, more fulfilling, and less complicated. Our challenges and problems will be easier to bear, and we will receive [God's] promised blessings. The knowledge which we seek, the answers for which we yearn, and the strength which we desire today to meet the challenges of a complex and changing world can be ours when we willingly obey the Lord's commandments."[9] Listen to the Savior's own words as He entreats us: "If ye love me, keep my commandments. . . . He that hath my commandments, and keepeth them, he it is that loveth me: and he that loveth me shall be loved of my Father, and I will love him, and will manifest myself to him" (John 14:15, 21).

May I suggest a further requisite in the continuing quest to finding the path of happiness? The golden pathway to happiness is one of selflessness and of giving love—the kind of love that has concern, interest, and some measure of charity for every living soul. That is true compassion. Striving to incorporate the Great Healer's art of compassion in ourselves is the direct route to the happiness that will enrich and bless our lives and the lives of others. It means that you show love even to your enemies, "bless them that curse you, do good to them that hate you, and pray for them which despitefully use you" (Matthew 5:44). In so doing, you will be fulfilling the greater commandment to love God Himself and to enjoy His love.

You will soar above the ill winds that blow, above the worldly, the self-defeating, and the bitter. You have the promise that "your whole bodies shall be filled with light, and there shall be no darkness in you; and that body which is filled with light comprehendeth all things" (Doctrine and Covenants 88:67). True and lasting happiness comes only when we choose to "love the Lord [our] God with all [our] heart, and with all [our] soul, and with all [our] might" (Deuteronomy 6:5).

May each one of us choose to love the Lord as we follow His paths for happiness. As we do, we will more fully feel the love of our Savior flowing into each moment of our lives.

CONCLUSION

Through the course of His life, the Savior showed unlimited capacity for compassion. He demonstrated it through His interactions with people no matter where He was, no matter what He might have been busy doing. He was never too busy or too distracted to love and serve those around Him. He blessed the little ones, healed the sick, comforted the mourners, raised the dead, cleansed repentant sinners, wept for unbelievers. He even forgave His crucifiers, and in one final act of unequaled compassion, He willingly offered His own perfect life to atone for the sins of mankind. Even while dying on the cross, Jesus forgot His own intense suffering and turned in compassion to His mother who had given Him life and who was weeping (see John 19:25–27).

The Savior has asked us to do the things that He has done, to bear one another's burdens, to comfort those who need comfort, to mourn with those who mourn, to feed the hungry, to visit the sick, to succor the weak, to lift up the hands that hang down, and to teach one another the doctrine of the kingdom (see Doctrine and Covenants 88:77). We are encouraged in the scriptures and by living prophets to find ways to be like Him. What better way to be like Him than to show compassion and love to those around us?

Our beloved Savior invites us to be His hands in helping, serving, and succoring those in need. He invites us to be His feet so that we might run to those who are in need of our help and service. He invites us to be His eyes so that we might always be looking for opportunities to serve. He invites us to be His ears so that we ever listen for those who might be crying out for help. He, in all His compassion and mercy, acted on behalf of those looking for physical, spiritual, or emotional healing. And in one way or another, we all will certainly at some point in our lives seek relief at the Savior's feet from our burdens, our sorrows, and our challenges. I promise you that our Savior is waiting for each of us to seek Him, that He might provide the relief we need. May we be motivated by the same feelings of compassion that the Lord has and act in mercy in behalf of those around us.

I witness that as we strive to incorporate this magnificent virtue of compassion into our lives, we will feel an unmeasured joy and satisfaction in our journey. Our capacity to serve others will enlarge, and our souls will be filled with a never-ending love for God and His children. I testify that when we genuinely show compassion to others, we will allow the atoning sacrifice of Christ to become wholly effective in our lives, and He will dwell in us and we in Him. As we love and serve our brothers and sisters, we will find ourselves becoming one with God and Jesus Christ.

ACKNOWLEDGMENTS

Though compassion is a subject I have been impressed to speak and write about for quite some time, these thoughts, impressions, and learnings would not have come together in a single volume without the help and support of many incredible people in my life. Indeed, this very book is a result of compassion shown toward me countless times as beloved family members, friends, associates, Church leaders, and the Lord Himself have extended patience, love, gentle teaching, and encouragement on this lifelong journey of discovering the Great Healer's art. This journey, I am confident, will be a continuing process for me.

For the past forty years, I have had the opportunity of witnessing firsthand what true, Christlike compassion looks like. Being such a loving, kind, and giving person, my wife Rosana has taught me more about what compassion means than I could have ever possibly learned on my own. I give thanks every day that the Lord, in His great mercy and love,

Acknowledgments

saw fit to bless me with a wife who could teach and love our family so completely. Some of the examples in this book include experiences I have had with my own children, who have also been great teachers to me. As with all things I have experienced and accomplished in my life, I would not be able to do what I do without the consistent, constant love and support of my family. They are so good to me, and I love and cherish them more than words can say.

Not only has my wife taught me through example, but she has also painstakingly assisted me in multiple word-for-word reviews of this manuscript, and her suggestions and feedback have been invaluable to me. I thank her for her contribution and for walking with me through this process. Additionally, I would like to thank my assistant Marianne Meyer, who has tirelessly helped me in the final revisions of this manuscript. I would also like to thank Casey Olson and his team for the many hours they have spent in reviewing the content of this book. Their doctrinal insights significantly strengthened the final product.

Of course, this acknowledgment must include recognition of the efforts of the fantastic and supportive Deseret Book staff: Laurel Day, Lisa Roper, Tracy Keck, Garth Bruner, and Rachael Ward. They took general ideas, feelings, and impressions, and helped turn this book into all it eventually became.

Acknowledgments

These great people are so gifted and talented in their respective roles.

I have striven to undertake this writing prayerfully, earnestly, and as guided by the promptings of the Spirit. As a disciple of Christ, I am continually offered opportunities to learn and grow and improve, and I recognize this journey as a process. As with any endeavor I undertake, my aim in this writing is to uphold the teachings of The Church of Jesus Christ of Latter-day Saints and share the gospel of Christ in a way that will draw others to Him. In case any errors are found within these pages, the fault lies with me and not with the Lord's gospel or His Church.

NOTES

Chapter 2: Joy and Peace in Him

1. "Peace in Christ," words and music by Nik Day, in *New Era*, Jan. 2018.
2. Russell M. Nelson, "This Easter, Find Peace in Jesus Christ," Mar. 28, 2021.
3. Russell M. Nelson, "Joy and Spiritual Survival," *Ensign*, Nov. 2016.
4. "Not Now, but in the Coming Years," translated from "Agora Não, mas Logo Mais," *Hymns* (Portuguese), no. 156.

Chapter 3: Being Meek and Lowly of Heart

1. Guide to the Scriptures, "Meek, Meekness."
2. *Preach My Gospel: A Guide to Missionary Service* (2004), 115.
3. Lorenzo Snow, in Conference Report, Apr. 1898, 13.
4. *Teachings of Presidents of the Church: Lorenzo Snow* (2012), 100–101.
5. Henry B. Eyring, "Families under Covenant," *Ensign*, May 2012.

Chapter 4: Ministering to All

1. See Russell M. Nelson, "Ministering," *Ensign*, May 2018, 100.

Chapter 5: Loving Those Who Are Different from Us

1. Marion G. Romney, "Man—A Child of God," *Ensign*, July 1973.

Notes

2. Russell M. Nelson, "Christ Is Risen; Faith in Him Will Move Mountains," *Liahona*, May 2021.

Chapter 6: Always Remember Him

1. Russell M. Nelson, in Russell M. Nelson and Wendy W. Nelson, "Hope of Israel," worldwide youth devotional, June 3, 2018; emphasis in original.
2. Wendy W. Nelson, in "Hope of Israel"; emphasis in original.
3. Uzziah, also known as Azariah; see 2 Kings 14:21; 15:1, 6–8; 1 Chronicles 3:12. See also 2 Chronicles 26.
4. See *Merriam-Webster*, s.v. "remember," http://www.merriam-webster.com/dictionary/remember.

Chapter 7: Learning and Teaching the Gospel

1. Russell M. Nelson, "Salvation and Exaltation," *Ensign*, May 2008, 9.

Chapter 8: Scriptures and Prophets: Testaments of Christ's Love

1. Joseph Smith, in "Minute Book 1," 44, josephsmithpapers.org; also at Church History Library, Salt Lake City; capitalization standardized.
2. Introduction to the Book of Mormon.
3. Introduction to the Book of Mormon; see also Moroni 10:3–5.
4. Introduction to the Book of Mormon.
5. Russell M. Nelson, "As We Go Forward Together," *Ensign*, Apr. 2018.
6. Neil L. Andersen, "The Prophet of God," *Ensign*, May 2018.

Chapter 9: The Gift of Repentance

1. Guide to the Scriptures, "Repent, Repentance."
2. Neil L. Andersen, "Repent . . . That I May Heal You," *Ensign*, Nov. 2009.

3. D. Todd Christofferson, "Recognizing God's Hand in Our Daily Blessings," *Ensign*, Jan. 2012.
4. *Teachings of Presidents of the Church: Joseph Smith* (2007), 48.
5. Russell M. Nelson, "We Can Do Better and Be Better," *Ensign*, May 2019.

Chapter 10: Taking Up Our Cross and Following Him

1. Bruce C. Hafen, *The Broken Heart: Applying the Atonement to Life's Experiences* (Salt Lake City: Deseret Book, 1989), 155–56.
2. See Neal A. Maxwell, "Repentance," *Ensign*, Nov. 1991, 32.

Chapter 11: Paths for Happiness

1. Gospel Topics, "Happiness," ChurchofJesusChrist.org.
2. In Conference Report, Oct. 1919, 180.
3. See John Helliwell, Richard Layard, and Jeffrey Sachs, eds., "World Happiness Report 2017," https://worldhappiness.report/ed/2017/.
4. "What Is Happiness?" *Psychology Today*, https://www.psychologytoday.com/basics/happiness.
5. "What Is Happiness?" *Psychology Today*, see https://www.psychologytoday.com/basics/happiness.
6. Russell M. Nelson, "Identity, Priority, and Blessings," *Ensign*, Aug. 2001.
7. Richard G. Scott, "Making the Right Decisions," *Ensign*, May 1991.
8. *Teachings of Presidents of the Church: Harold B. Lee* (2000), 176, 178.
9. Thomas S. Monson, "Keep the Commandments," *Ensign*, Nov. 2015.

IMAGE CREDITS

vi: kuarmungadd/Adobe Stock
4: Carlos Santa Maria/Adobe Stock
9: Rawpixel.com/Adobe Stock
11: Antonioguillem/Adobe Stock
14: Jacob Lund/Adobe Stock
16: Viacheslav Yakobchuk/Adobe Stock
21: tutye/Adobe Stock
25: sanderstock/Adobe Stock
29: manusapon/Adobe Stock
32: inews77/Adobe Stock
37: fizkes/Adobe Stock
40: arrowsmith2/Adobe Stock
42: JHDT Productions/Adobe Stock
47: Evgeniy Kalinovskiy/Adobe Stock
52: pahis/Adobe Stock
56: Photographee.eu/Adobe Stock
60: Synthex/Adobe Stock
65: Halfpoint/Adobe Stock
69: Antonioguillem/Adobe Stock
72: sewcream/Adobe Stock
77: mimagephotos/Adobe Stock
81: sebra/Adobe Stock
86: saksit/Adobe Stock
93: Halfpoint/Adobe Stock
96: Wirestock/Adobe Stock
100: Kalani/Adobe Stock
105: sebra/Adobe Stock
108: Laci/Adobe Stock
112: Sonate/Adobe Stock
116: kieferpix/Adobe Stock
120: digitalskillet1/Adobe Stock
125: Wirestock/Adobe Stock
128: rawpixel.com/Adobe Stock
134: Antonioguillem/Adobe Stock
138: Sabphoto/Adobe Stock
141: jovannig/Adobe Stock
144: 300816975/Adobe Stock
146: candy1812/Adobe Stock
149: Miramiska/Adobe Stock
152: Inga Pracute/Adobe Stock
155: rjankovsky/Adobe Stock
158: Krakenimages.com/Adobe Stock
160: fizkes/Adobe Stock